Inclusion...
It's Not Just an
Educational Buzzword

The Being, Knowing and Doing of Education

Dianne McConnell Ph.D

Tellwell Talent
www.tellwell.ca

ISBN
978-0-2288-9182-6 (Hardcover)
978-0-2288-9181-9 (Paperback)
978-0-2288-9183-3 (eBook)

Dedication

In loving memory of my beautiful boys, Erik and Ben. The world is a better place because of you. You are champions for the messages of inclusive practice. Your journey laid the foundation of hope, inspiration, and passion for those who are paying attention to this call to action.

To my amazing, beautiful, handsome life partner. You are my soulmate and love of my life; I am so grateful.

To my gorgeous and incredible daughter whom I love dearly, her husband, and my adorable grandson Chephren. You make my heart full.

Friends, family, and colleagues, thank you for your presence; you have made my life rich beyond belief.

A special shout-out to my good friend Steve Cairns. Your passion and support encouraged and inspired me. Your brilliant insights and feedback over the many times you read the manuscript added tremendous value to the story, and I am so grateful and lucky to have had the opportunity to work on this project with you walking beside me.

Finally, to all of you who are reading this book, and thinking about the experience others have in your presence.

Table of Contents

Acknowledgements

I would sincerely like to thank Tellwell Publishing and team for the opportunity and the support that has been provided for me on this journey. Thank you, team, I deeply appreciate all that you have done and continue to do.

Thank you to those very special individuals who so graciously accepted my invitation to read my work and provided me with the wonderful reflections and thoughts on their experience of reading the book. I am so filled with gratitude that I am blessed with knowing such beautiful people like you.

Thank you, Steve, for your very thoughtful and inspirational words in the Foreword. Our community is so much richer because of your presence. I am so grateful to have the privilege of our friendship.

Thank you to the "hope carriers" in my life; I am surrounded by you, and you know who you are. My friends, family members, co-workers, colleagues, and acquaintances who inspired me, encouraged me, supported me, and moved me forward to complete my dream of writing a second book. You have made a difference in my life. Thank you.

Thank you to my amazing family. I love you deeply.

Foreword

Dianne is destined to become a superstar in the transformation of education.

Those who become the best in their field are often seen by others to have something special. Their skills, knowledge, character, and energy combine to be more than the sum of those parts. The superstars in sports, arts, sciences, politics possess an oversized talent, but are often unaware of their uniqueness. As those gifted and talented individuals rise to greatness, they leave the rest of us in awe of the quantitative and qualitative evidence that follows in their wake. Their achievements inspire and motivate others to challenge themselves, to emulate the exceptional, to nurture and perpetuate the new level of what can be, must be, and (most notably) already has been accomplished.

With quiet humility, Dianne is emerging in the field of education as a leader in the change process that will bring equity and inclusion to schools, school communities, and the systemic practice of education in our society. This is coming at a time when transforming the "why and how" of educating our children is existentially vital to our global village.

"If I have seen further [than others], it is by standing on the shoulders of giants."[1]

Dianne has earned her authority through years of research and the implementation of the beliefs, knowledge, and application of

---

[1] Isaac Newton, *"Letter from Sir Isaac Newton to Robert Hooke"*, (Historical Society of Pennsylvania; retrieved 7 June, 2018).

inclusion in education, but what makes Dianne's work significant is the fact that one of the *"shoulders of giants"* that she has stood upon, was her own. That may be difficult to envision, but the reader of *Inclusion: Not Just an Educational Buzzword!* will appreciate the importance of this comment, as Dianne's experiences are revealed through her professional and personal journey with the realities of inclusion for herself and her three children.

Following a serendipitous meeting with Dianne, we soon discovered that my personal and professional life experiences as a parent, innovative educator, and school administrator dovetailed with Dianne's experiences as a mother and educator. Typical of Dianne's character, I soon had a draft of this book. I began framing Dianne's work through a lens of inclusion that was founded on the work of child developmental psychologist, Dr. Gordon Neufeld. Supporting Dianne's work through my experience in a school environment that was founded on the beliefs, knowing, and application of inclusion, Dianne's work will inspire, energize, and guide a transition to inclusionary practice in schools, communities, and the larger systems within which they exist.

Steven Cairns BA., MEd
Retired School Administrator

Endorsements

This book should come with a warning that the contents of this book may ache your heart, challenge your beliefs, and yet also support us as we revise and shift inclusive practices. Readers should have tissues and a notepad in hand as they dive in. This book is an invitation to delve into a thought-provoking journey that will challenge your beliefs and touch your heart.

Dr. McConnell's book on inclusion caught my attention even before I opened the first page, due to her inspiring reputation and personal stories of raising two sons with disabilities. I had the privilege of hearing her speak in person and was moved by her experiences with her sons, Ben and Erik, and her family. I had no idea that the words on the page could still evoke such strong emotions on the topic of inclusion. Her impactful stories are a true inspiration, and I am grateful for the role she plays in making classrooms more inclusive and caring for all students.

This book—the stories shared and support given—are a true testament to the power of belief and action. I could not put the book down, and it has reminded me that our beliefs and actions can have a profound impact on creating a more inclusive and caring world. She gives us support on the being, knowing, and doing aspects of education. I have never had a book evoke such emotions yet give such support to our practice. I highly recommend this read for all teachers, educators, parents, and leaders.

Thank you! It was a pleasure to read this book!

Rhae-Ann Holoien, Superintendent,
Buffalo Trail School Division

Dr. McConnell writes from the heart. But she also writes from the lived experience of a parent and an education leader. She sees a future in which we, as a coordinated community, educate and support our youth through principled collaboration. She urges us to work as community partners, with compassion, focus, purpose, and shared knowledge. This book compels educators and service providers to examine our principles and values; not just our data. Dianne's vision for a child-focused and collaborative education and support model demands our attention.

Nina Wyrostok PhD

Dianne's writing embodies deep wisdom, through a rare insight encompassing a holistic lens of belief, intellect, and behavior. While impressive in current research, knowledge, and actions required in advancing an inclusive system, Dianne's unique lived experiences and reflection as a mother, educator, scholar, and leader, compels us into the unchartered territory of *being* in a profound way not yet examined. This book demands personal reflection, and empowers leaders to dig deeper into their own context, including courageously challenging the deep waters of their belief system and identity, essential for individual and systemic change in the evolution of inclusion. A truly powerful call to action.

Loriann Steinwand, MEd

I was fortunate to work with Dianne when she was well established in her journey to improve the lives of all students through inclusive practices, and I am a better person for it. This book reflects the work I was able to bear witness to and take part in with Dianne, as she weaves research, current classroom realities, and her steadfast will to create a space of belonging for all students in our schools. Dianne seamlessly walks the reader through her own powerful story, policy, and practice in a way that develops a compelling "why" for her call to action. May we all be, know, and do better.

Dr. Garette Tebay, Superintendent, Saskatchewan Rivers Public School Division

I just finished reading your glorious book! Congratulations once again! Your insight, lived experience, willingness to be vulnerable in order to connect with your readers, knowledge, passion, and intelligence all shine through in spades! I am impressed with the way you interweave intellectual concepts with personal stories in order to assist readers in understanding the concepts that you are presenting. You lay out a vision and blueprint for achieving inclusion (the how) that is thoroughly supported by all the reasons that this vision and blueprint need to come to fruition. You help your readers to not only understand, but to buy into and connect emotionally with the concept of inclusion and all the possibility it holds. It is a perfect encore to "Could This Be Grace?"

Kathryn Graff, MEd, Educational Consultant

Dr. Dianne McConnell is a passionate, committed, educational leader who is passionate about community building and self-inquiry. Her writing reflects the experience of a woman who has spent years learning from and with children, teachers, learning leaders and elected officials. She provides stories, tools and years of experience that allow us to ask ourselves one of her favorite questions: "What's the end in mind for this work in school communities?" This book will allow you to explore your own personal and professional journey while connecting it to healthy, inclusive learning spaces and to source answers to her question with new insight.

Felica Ochs, MEd, Change Health Alberta, Executive Director

Preface

I recently retired from a career in education. I have a PhD in Special Education, and am a registered psychologist. My work included being Director of Student Services and lead supervisor of "Setting the Direction—Initiative for Inclusion" for the Province of Alberta, and Associate School District Superintendent. I have been involved in the field as a teacher, consultant, administrator, senior leader within government, and executive team member within a school division.

I was fortunate to have three beautiful children, two boys and a girl. My two sons were born prematurely and continued to experience health challenges as they grew. When my youngest son was diagnosed with a severe visual impairment, the reality of parenting a child that was blind terrified me. My focus in education shifted, and I became increasingly alarmed with what was and what was not happening within education to support children with diverse needs. Consequently, my efforts quickly became focused on special education and inclusion.

Many have adopted an understanding of inclusion that is embedded in the special education world, describing a process of programming for all students in "typical" classrooms. I have since learned that true inclusion is a call to action for being human and feeling safe enough to express one's vulnerability. I heard this call to action as the disease in Ben's eyes progressed and it became evident to us that he was going to lose his vision at 2 years of age. My fear drove me back to university in search of the acquisition of skills and knowledge to assist me in coping with my situation. I believed that if I discovered or designed the right resource, the right strategy or support for Ben, he could acquire the skills necessary to appear as a sighted individual. What I learned during my doctoral research was that Ben was never going to be a sighted person, and in fact, my quest to find a means for him to appear so was robbing me of the important time of really getting to know, accept, and embrace my son. His world was different from mine, and when I realized that and heard the call, I slowed down, became curious and fostered the development of a welcoming, supportive, and loving relationship.

Throughout the years, I noticed that my views about inclusion had changed. I was influenced by the research, but most importantly I was impacted by parenting two boys with very significant needs and a healthy daughter impacted by the degree of adversity in our family. As a result of deep reflection and personal work, I came to understand the value and importance of *connecting* with our children in a manner that nurtured a deep sense of *belonging*. My eldest son Erik suffered from a very serious necrotic hip that caused him tremendous suffering as a result of severe pain. He became addicted to pain medication, developed serious mental health issues and a hip infection that created a two-year stay in hospital. I was aware of his growing isolation, depression, and sense of hopelessness, but I was ill equipped at the time with an understanding of how to show up for him. Ben, on the other hand, suffered many of the same health challenges without the complication of severe pain. His life was full of opportunity, relationships, and support; as a result, I have many stories of his successful life experiences. Ben developed a strong sense of self and I believe it had to do with his experience of belonging.

My daughter, the eldest of the three, was vibrant and healthy throughout this journey and it was not until years later and much reflection on my part that I recognized the sense of disconnect and isolation that was created for her as a result of our focus on the failing health of her brothers. Dr. Gordon Neufeld is a strong advocate for Attachment Theory [2] as the foundation of a healthy

---

[2] Roots of Attachment public webinar *https://neufeldinstitute.org/resources/free/*

relationship that can establish a sense of belonging. He states that it is never too late to make a connection with one's children to create a sense of belonging. I take heart in believing that I can now come 'alongside' our 40-year-old daughter to connect with her as she struggles to understand and cope with her wounded emotions and negative self-talk.

After my sons passed away, in 2017 and 2019, I reflected on our journey and published a book called *Could This Be Grace? A question that helps us gain strength and see opportunity in the face of adversity,* which is about the insights and lessons I learned as a result of my experience of our family journey. My hope was that the lessons I had learned, and that changed my professional practice and my view of being a mother, would be applicable to other parents, teachers, and health care providers. The transformative experience I had gifted upon me gave me the insights to see possibility and opportunity in the face of adversity. I felt that I could see the light of our situation and feel grateful for the experience.

I have continued to think about inclusion and inclusive practice and have come to realize that inclusion should **not** be an educational buzzword. It is not a place, a practice, a process, or an initiative; rather, I believe that it must be a call to action to change our pedagogical practice and ultimately our educational system to embrace diversity and instill in **every** student a sense of self-worth, connection, and belonging.

This book is based on my personal experiences as an education professional and parent. I have spent my entire career working in Alberta as a teacher, educational psychologist, administrator, and bureaucrat, so my examples and thoughts are specific to those experiences. My views on inclusion and inclusive practice emerged from observation, experience, and the research that underpinned my doctoral dissertation. I have included references to educational documents and authors who have influenced me along the way.

Introduction

Buzzwords in Education

According to the Oxford Dictionary[3], *buzzword* is defined as "A word or phrase, often an item of jargon that is fashionable at a particular time or in a particular context."

On Kathleen Trace's website[4] she outlines twenty-seven education buzzwords that prospective educators should know in 2022. Examples include asynchronous/synchronous learning, data-driven teaching, equality vs equity, growth mindset, **inclusion**, innovative inquiry, mindfulness, project-based learning, student-centred learning, student choice, and voice and social-emotional learning.

---

[3] *https://www.oxfordlearnersdictionaries.com/definition/english/buzzword*
[4] *http://www.wannabeteacher.com*

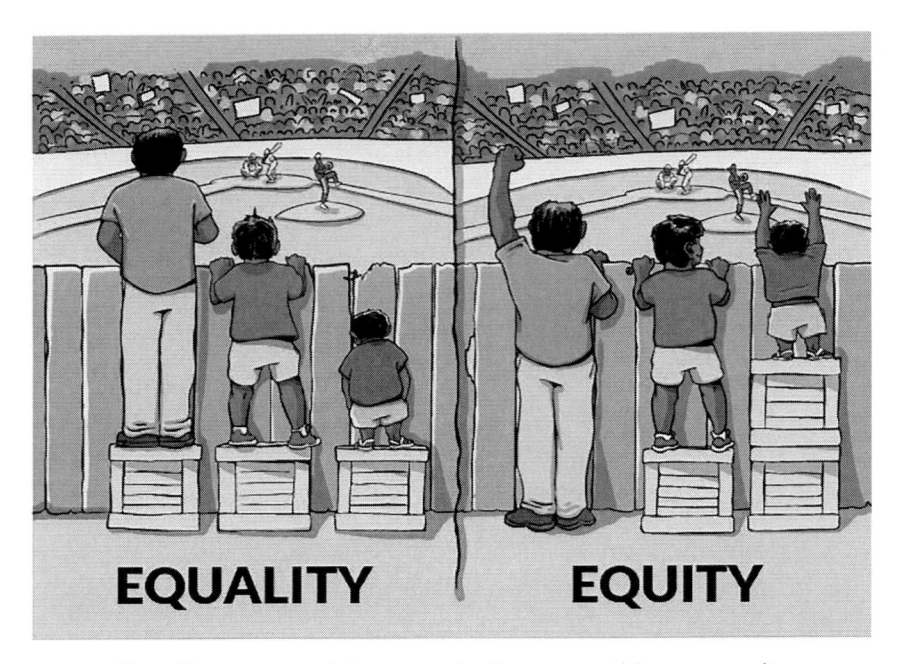

Equality means giving people the same thing vs equity which means creating fairness in every situation (permission to reproduce from interaction institute for social change, artist Angus Maguire).

Educational buzzwords are constantly changing and appear to follow a certain pattern. Early in my career I noticed that each school year would herald a new initiative with a unique set of words, phrases, and acronyms with the clearly stated expectation that this "new way" would be incorporated into the existing practice. Despite in-service training opportunities (that varied in accordance with available financial and human resources), experience soon revealed that one could avoid anxiety by simply waiting for next year's "new thing." Inclusion shows up on Kathleen Trace's list of educational buzzwords for 2022.

I do not believe that inclusion is a buzzword. The word inclusion has been evolving over time and has come to mean different things to different people, depending on their lived experience with diversity. Over time, our understanding of the meaning of inclusion has changed.

Think of the word inclusion as a call to action—a call for all of us to think about our relationships, think about how we engage with others, think about how our behaviors and decisions impact others. Overtime, this call to action has become louder and louder and I believe individuals are seriously considering how to respond.

To fully understand this call to action I believe it is important to understand the historical evolution of education that has been fueled by societal changes and expectations. We need to establish clarity and agreement—not only about what an education system that is inclusive looks like, but clarity and understanding about what our relationship with diversity is. Of course, we need to be clear about what evidence needs to be gathered to promote confidence that our system is delivering on an inclusive education agenda.

Philosophically, folks don't disagree with the definition of inclusive education that has been proposed. They fully support the ideals and agree, "Yes, that is the sort of environment in which I would like to live and work." So . . . why isn't it happening? We need to understand the problems of practice, examine the root cause (because the problems of practice will be the symptoms), and develop an action plan to address the root cause. I see that the work of authentically transforming educational environments to become inclusive has three important steps: being, knowing, and doing within our educational practice.

My personal life has taken me on a journey that created opportunities for me to reconsider my relationship with understanding of diversity and to rethink how I showed up in the world. The lessons I learned in my personal life influenced my thinking in my professional life as an educator and I am now more clearly able to see inclusion as a call to action.

This book examines the evolution of the word inclusion, clarifies the meaning of the word, introduces some key thoughts about what is getting in the way of implementing inclusive environments, collecting evidence, and being, knowing, and doing in educational practice. I have woven through the chapters the lessons I learned from my personal experience as a parent; I am hoping they will offer a unique perspective.

The time is **now,** and this call to action is for you.

Chapter One

THE EVOLUTION OF INCLUSION

I have followed the work of Mike Dooley and taken his training and became an "Infinite Possibilities Trainer." During the course Mike Dooley taught us that our beliefs come first, and those beliefs influence our thoughts, words, and actions, and then the world around us. **I learned that your beliefs create your experience.** Mike shared with us that beliefs are why people succeed in sports, music, business, and everything else. An example he gave us was the Wright brothers. He told us that if they did not believe that it was possible to fly then they could have never dream about the possibility and then actually flew. A continuing theme throughout the course was about the connection of our beliefs and our life and to understand that beliefs can be changed.

An illustration of my transformation of beliefs begins with my experience as a first-year teacher, teaching Grade 3. I was trained in the processes and strategies of delivering educational materials and I *believed* that my job as a teacher was to have learned how to deliver these materials well. I loved my students and welcomed them into my class each day. I cared about their accomplishments, their interests, and their passions. I was there to support them in their struggles. Things were good.

One day in the early fall I was introduced to a new student that was being placed in my room. I was told that this little girl had never been in a school before and had never been exposed to reading or writing. She did not know about the alphabet and did not know her colors. Her story was tragic. She had been moved from foster family to foster family and up to this point had only experienced a life filled with uncertainty, poverty, and trauma. She was not well.

I panicked—I did not know what to do. I had no tools in my toolbox to support this little girl. I knew that I was not going to do a good job teaching her, or at least that was how I felt. After all, I was not trained, I had no experience. At this time, I was strongly influenced by my training of delivering the curriculum well. This little girl deserved better than what I had to offer—someone better than me at providing what she needed. I believed that **she should not be in my classroom.**

I honestly believed that my decision to exclude this child from my classroom was in her best interest. I cared about her and believed that a child with her needs would not learn from me, because I believed that I needed to have the training and expertise to teach a child with profound needs. I must have learned early on in my life that to do something well you must have training.

According to Miguel Ruiz in his book *The Four Agreements* he equates our belief system to a Book of Law that rules our mind. He goes on to say that without question, whatever is in that Book of Law, is our truth and we base all our judgements according to our Book of Law. Our beliefs influence and govern our behaviors and the decisions we make.

David Irvine is a thought leader, author, speaker, teacher, and coach whom I have admired and followed over the past couple of years. He has written several books and offers courses in which he teaches the principles of authentic leadership. When I took David's master class based on his book, *The Other Everest,* I was able to see that my training as a teacher instilled in me a belief that my job was to deliver a quality program to my students. I believed it was important to pay attention to pedagogy and outcomes and that therein lay the measure of my success. Of course, I had my students' best interests at heart—IF they fit into my belief about my role as a teacher and IF they fit into my belief about my relationship with diversity. Through my work with David Irvine, I learned that my belief with respect to diversity and my students was transactional in nature. Transactional relationships focus on tasks, measures, controlling, planning, and knowing. Diversity threatened my view of feeling successful in my job. David taught me that transformational relationships focus on presence, dreams, inspiration, purpose, and connection with others. Transformational relationships embody "being."

Embracing transformational relationships is foundational in an education system that is inclusive. We will know that the educational system we are operating in is inclusive and inclusive practices have become embedded in the culture when the term itself becomes obsolete. We would no longer see designations of "inclusion classroom," "inclusion student," or "inclusion school." Consider that the term "inclusive education" survives if we continue to believe that some of our students do not belong in our classrooms or schools.

The belief stated in the previous sentence sat in my "Book of Law" and was my truth.

Miguel Ruiz and his son José Ruiz published a second book, *The Fifth Agreement.* Their teachings tell us to become skeptical, introspective, and to listen because perhaps what we have agreed to is not true—it is only true because we agreed to it. Since our belief systems govern our behaviors and decisions, it made sense to me that our relationship with diversity evolves and changes as our belief about the possibilities and potential of diversity changes.

Inclusive education researcher and educator, Shelly Moore has a YouTube video titled *The Evolution of Inclusion*[5]. She points out that inclusion has been evolving over many years, and illustrates this through a graphic of green and colored dots, with the green dots representing typical students and colored dots representing

---

[5] Shelley Moore, "The Evolution of Inclusion," October 1, 2018, presentation, 5:03, *https://www.youtube.com/watch?v=PQgXBhPh5Zo.*

students with diverse needs. Initially, society's belief about children with special or diverse needs was that they required specialized placement, with specialized supports and services. This aligned with the belief that I had as a Grade 3 teacher regarding the little girl with profound needs—a belief that this student's needs would be best met with people that are trained and know how best to support her learning needs. As a result, specialized educational placements or institutionalized settings existed. Also, at the time perhaps supporting students with special or diverse needs was expensive and as a result moving them to specialized settings was more cost effective. I believe that the decisions made at this time were made based on what decision-makers believed to be true, and that these decisions were made with the best interest of students in mind. However, the consequence was that these settings excluded them from their peers and community.

As education evolved, new beliefs regarding special needs and diversity emerged. More and more individuals challenged the belief that students with special or diverse needs had to receive their education in an isolated setting, and as a result schools began to develop programs within the school to serve these students. The students were no longer excluded from their community and their community schools, although they were segregated within the school building. There were now special education classrooms, resource rooms, and resource rooms for special education teachers.

As special education research emerged, belief systems were influenced, creating a shift from special education classrooms or programs to integrating these students into mainstream classrooms. At that time, in Alberta, school jurisdictions had the opportunity to identify students requiring special education supports or services, prepare a file demonstrating that the student met Alberta Education criteria for special education support, and submit the documentation in hopes that the file would be approved and funding would follow. This process was rigorous and required assessments from professionals specializing in the identification of special education needs.

Gathering this information through the required specialized assessments was challenging because these assessments were expensive and involved extensive administrative support. Also, parents were starting to create some resistance and tension based on their interpretation that they were being asked to provide information outlining how badly their child needed supports in order to trigger funding for those supports.

In 2000, the Minister of Education was becoming aware of the shift in belief systems and an increasing pressure for change. As a result, a Special Education Review called *Shaping the Future* was initiated, to review the delivery of educational programs and services for students with special needs. The review resulted in several recommendations in key areas, but also recommended a need for provincial policy in the areas of early identification and screening, transition planning, and cross-government joint service plans for students with special education needs. The report identified the importance of parental involvement in the children's education, in Alberta Learning, and in providing resources.

Education, not only in Alberta and Canada but worldwide, has reflected and been responsive to societal needs, advancements in technology and social media, globalization, environmental issues, ease of travel, and socio-economic pressures. Government's responsibility is to be responsive to these factors and incorporate policies and beliefs to reflect changes.

In 2010 Sir Ken Robinson provided an illustration of how education responds to societal needs in a TED talk he gave called *The Changing Paradigm of Education*[6].

In this talk he points out that the Industrial Revolution created the need for people to work in factories—people who could follow directions and do repetitive work all day as a means of supporting themselves, but also because they were told it was

---

[6] Ken Robinson, "The Changing Paradigm of Education," October 14, 2010, presentation, 11:40, *https://www.ted.com/talks/ sir ken robinson changing education paradigms*.

their contribution to making their society better. Education responded by creating an educational system where students learned the basics by memorization, followed a schedule dictated by bells, and did repetitive learning activities.

Sir Ken Robinson challenged the way we educate our children, championing a radical rethink of how our school systems cultivate creativity and acknowledge multiple types of intelligence. At the same time, I believe that society has also created some tension and pressures regarding how the education system responds to diverse learning needs.

As society's opinions of how individuals with diverse needs change with respect to how they are viewed within our community, education has a responsibility to incorporate and reflect these changes and demands within their system. A common view is that education has not kept pace with societal changes, as Sir Ken Robinson's message points out.

In 2002, Alberta initiated its first in-depth examination of its education system in more than thirty years. The idea for this review came from stakeholder groups suggesting that a comprehensive review would guide plans and better align education to societal trends. This report, titled *Every child learns, every child succeeds: report and recommendations*, provided the government with ninety-four recommendations for systemic change and began the conversation about the need to transform the education system.

In June of 2004, the Alberta Government published *Standards for Special Education, amended June 2004*. The School Act outlined the rights and responsibilities of students identified with special education needs and required boards to provide resident students with access to special education programs. *The Standards for Special Education, amended June 2004,* requires school boards to identify and deliver effective programming for students identified with special education needs. The document was intended to provide assurance to society that students identified with special education needs received appropriate quality programming consistent with their peers.

To provide clarity for appropriate quality programming for students identified with a low-incidence disability, the government provided companion documents for the standards called *Essential Components for Educational Programming.* A low-incidence disability is one in which very few individuals have been identified; examples include blindness or visual impairment, deafness or hard of hearing, and the autism spectrum. An essential component document was written for each of these low-incidence disabilities.

As the years passed, Alberta continued to focus on finding the best ways to deliver programming for students identified with diverse needs. In the fall of 2007, the government involved school boards in a provincial review of special education identification and funding processes. As a result of that review, the government decided to engage Albertans in a discussion about the future of special education in the province and called this initiative "Setting the Direction." The result of that engagement initiative was the development of an education framework describing an inclusive education system. The review committee heard Albertans talk about special education as a siloed system running parallel to the education system and emphasized the need for **one education system** designed to serve all students.

In 2013, the government appended a *Ministerial Order on Learning* to the *School Act* to emphasize student learning. A year later, prompted by ongoing concerns about the state of inclusion in Alberta, the Alberta Teachers Association passed a resolution to strike a Blue Ribbon Panel on Inclusive Education in Alberta Schools to provide an arm's-length comprehensive review on this topic.

Although the public generally embraced the philosophy of inclusive education, concerns were expressed about the capacity and support for implementation. The purpose of the review was to focus on support for implementation of inclusive education. The findings in the report included an expressed need for more research and information on program delivery within inclusive environments and the need to support implementation with funding and resources.

From the time the educational system developed during the Industrial Revolution, as Sir Ken Robinson points out, to the present day, our beliefs about diversity have been changing. As a result, our education system has changed and evolved, reflecting these new beliefs. Today, it is fair to say that many educators believe that all students can learn, and that diversity is an asset.

We recognize that education is inclusive if there are high expectations for all students, and the environments are safe, supportive, and caring. Teachers have available to them a continuum of supports and services and work collaboratively with their partners, and there is a plan to support teachers and ensure that they have the capacity to deliver on the agenda of education that is inclusive. For example, in 2019, a movement occurred in Alberta to put standards of practice[7] in place for system leaders and superintendents, to ensure that they had the competencies for instructional leadership and the professional development to support the skill development of competencies.

A common thread through the evolution of inclusion has been the realization that relationship and connection are a vital component of an educational system that is inclusive. Therefore, "being" is an important element in the personal and systemic shifts necessary to accomplish this work. Until recently, I had not thought about "being" as an important piece in the evolution of inclusive practice, which begs the important question: how does *being* fit into the meaning of inclusion?

---

[7] Alberta Education, *Superintendent Leadership Quality Standard,* (Edmonton, Alberta: Alberta Education, 2020), *https://open.alberta.ca/publications/ superintendent-leadership-quality-standard-2020*

Chapter Two

HOW DOES BEING FIT WITH INCLUSIVE PRACTICE?

At one year of age, my youngest child was diagnosed with a retinal disease unfamiliar to the doctors in Edmonton and he was referred to the Massachusetts Eye and Ear Infirmary in Boston. Over the course of two years, we made thirty-one trips with him for eye surgeries; the eventual result was that he had his eyes removed. I was super panicked (which is way bigger than just panicked) and had two thoughts:

- I was not trained; and
- I did not know what to do.

Unlike my experience as a teacher, where I could logically conclude that the student did not belong in my class until I had acquired the knowledge and skills to meet the child's needs, I could not say that my son did not belong in my family! Oh dear . . . I needed a plan.

My situation was painful, scary—no, *beyond* scary, terrifying—so I asked myself, "If this was my student and I had to be the teacher, what would I do?" I did not ask, "What would a mom do?" I was asking myself a head question because the heart question was too painful.

The teacher's question took me on a journey back to university to figure out how a teacher would support a student with blindness, and it was not until I did my doctoral research that I found the answer—and it was profound. It was not about what would the teacher DO. It was not about the doing. It was about how the teacher would BE—it was about relationship and connection. And then the miracle happened—I asked myself how this applies to my role as a mom, and when I reflected on that; I was able to see that I was so busy *doing* that I failed to see my boy, failed to be curious about his world, failed to make an authentic connection with him.

So began my journey to a better understanding of *being*. My relationship with diversity was changing. I realized that I could accept the fact that I did not know what to do and gave myself permission to be vulnerable, curious, and welcoming.

Shelley Moore acknowledged that she was not quite there yet, when she depicted her initial graphic of inclusion with the colored dots interspersed with the green dots. In her book, *One Without the Other*, she tells the story of the day when one of her students challenged her with the thought that if inclusion is a **belief** that every individual is unique, why would you have green dots at all? So, inclusive practice is as much about how we show up—what one believes and knows—as it is about what we do. It is a belief about how one views diversity, which is reflected in one's decisions and behaviors when faced with diversity.

To date, I believe inclusion is more focused on what one does—that is, programming and placement—than on one's beliefs and understanding of what inclusive practice could and should be. I have illustrated the point that inclusion has been evolving over many years and education has responded to societal needs throughout that evolution. Some, especially parents and special interest groups, would say that the response from education has not been quick enough, that we still have a distance to go to achieve what society wants inclusive practices to be. I agree that we still have a distance to go, but I feel that we are now on the cusp of change and are better prepared to have a transformational shift in education that will bring inclusive practice to all students.

In Chapter 1, I mentioned the provincial initiative, "Setting the Direction", where the provincial government asked Albertans to respond to the question, "What do you think/want special education to look like?" The consistent response was "We want education to be inclusive and equitable for all. Our current special education system is a well-designed system running parallel to our education system. When our children and students are identified as needing special education, they get disenfranchised from the education system and in most cases never return." In response to these societal views, Alberta Education established an inclusive education policy.

> **"Inclusion is a way of thinking and acting that demonstrates universal acceptance and promotes a sense of belonging for all learners."** [8]

Our society has been talking about inclusion for a long time, and as a result the word itself has become as much of a barrier as it has been helpful. I say this because the inclusion journey has been interpreted differently at different points in time. Therefore, what often happens is that when we are engaged in a conversation about inclusion, we may each have a different interpretation of what the word means, so we may end up not talking about the same thing.

So, what does inclusive practice really mean? I suggest that our belief system with respect to diversity has not evolved to reflect the intent of the *knowing* and *doing* of educational practice that is inclusive. We might see some shifts in practice, the *doing*, but at

---

[8] https://www.alberta.ca/guide-to-education.aspx

the end of the day have we really understood and embraced what it means to **be** within an inclusive environment? One must become curious about the learners' way of engaging with the content and one must authentically connect with each learners' style.

An essential understanding of inclusion is that *being* and *doing* inclusion becomes the natural way in which we work. The *being* piece of this work is the most difficult to get our heads around. I think of the *being* piece as how you show up in front of your students. **What is the experience that students have from being in your presence?** It is about relationships. Being human requires you to become vulnerable and not allow your own feelings of inadequacy to create a barrier between you and another individual.

During the time I was working on my doctoral dissertation my advisor, Dr. Dick Sobsey, from the University of Alberta, gave me permission to publish this poem he had written about his experience with disability.

My Child: An Introduction

When the little boy on the bus held back his
tears, people said he was brave.
When my child does the same thing, a doctor tells me
that "retarded children are insensitive to pain,
When the little girl who lives next door fought
for her rights, people called her assertive.
When my child does the same thing, a behavioral psychologist
tells me that "retarded children are noncompliant."
When other children suffer, people look for
ways to make their lives happier.
When children like mine suffer, bioethicists ask
if it might not be better to end their lives.
Professionals tell me that I am grieving
. . . grieving for my disabled child
. . . grieving for the loss of the healthy child that I wished for
. . . grieving for something irretrievably lost

I need not grieve for my child, perfect in his own way.
My sorrow is for those who cast dark professional
shadows and fail to see my child's light.

This poem represents experiences with a child who has significant disabilities, from two different perspectives. I would argue that these two perspectives likely hold true in views held about *diversity.*

The first perspective may be held by individuals who have never had close personal experiences with disabilities or various diversities. As a result, their expectations evolve from a belief system that has been influenced by a lack of information, or inappropriate information. Possibly, they have had uncomfortable or negative experiences that prevented them from hoping or believing that diversity could have rewarding moments. This perspective may also be held by individuals who have had experiences with disabilities or diversity and are informed, but only consider the disability and forget about the individuals and their families.

When my son was very young and we were first introduced to the fact that he was going to be blind I was involved with professionals that fell into this first category illustrated in the poem. I allowed professionals to make decisions on behalf of my child at the school level. I allowed professionals to accompany me to the doctor's office and ask the questions. I allowed professionals to tell us that our home was not in a safe location and we should consider moving. When I asked the doctor for information about whether I should be in contact with services or agencies as our son's vision deteriorated, I was told they would tell me when it was time. They were going to be the ones to decide for us. At the time, I was accepting of this place, this position in which I found myself. I felt that I was not able to challenge or question them, because I was afraid of jeopardizing access to services for my son. I focused on the perceived benefits to him and swallowed my own feelings and concerns about our situation.

My husband and I met a fine doctor in Boston who practiced medicine from the second perspective. When we visited Dr. Walton we expected to be told briefly, in medical terms, about our son's condition. Instead, we met an individual who always talked about our home, our jobs, our other children. He asked so many questions about the other children that he began to know them, even at that distance. He asked us how we were managing. He asked us what kind of support and resources were available at home. When we told him we did not have any information, he sent us a book in the mail. In the hospital he had a reputation among the staff comparable to a knight in shining armour. He left orders not to wake children at night. His orders always included items that would enhance the comfort and total well-being of the child and family; for example, having humidifiers by their beds, and removing IVs before children came out of anaesthesia. He truly exemplified the second perspective in the poem.

I consider myself very fortunate to have had a profound personal experience in my life that exemplifies what *being* for the child and family looks like, feels like, and the difference it makes for all involved. It is not a story from education, but it is a wonderful example of what we are striving to achieve for all our students.

My two boys suffered from a very unforgiving genetic disorder. They faced significant challenges throughout their lives, and as a family we moved from one specialist to another, from one hospital ward to another, and from one system to another. Throughout their journey our family was challenged by gaps in the system, walls between mandates, and always, always protocols, processes, and procedures.

In October 2019, our youngest son, then thirty-two, was admitted to the intensive care unit of the hospital. His doctor was one of the intensivists in the unit. She connected with us regularly and always approached us with a broader view and interest beyond just her patient, our son. Just before Christmas, a decision was made that our son was not going to be coming home. She had the conversation with him in a gentle, compassionate way. Shortly after that, on a Friday night she showed up with a specimen bottle with his name on it, filled with a special drink; she had a syringe and a special drink in her other hand. She announced that it was "a special time" and she brought special drinks for both because (of course) he could not celebrate alone. She set the rules—no hospital talk, just good stories.

After Christmas, treatment stopped. Hospital protocol dictates that when patients are no longer receiving acute care (in other words, treatment) you cannot stay in the active treatment unit—you must be moved. The next thing we experienced was a visit from a doctor that we had never met. She introduced herself to us as "the facilitator of end-of-life." She was there to talk to us about our son's death—how it would be, what he could expect. She told him, "You are dying, and you cannot stay here. We are moving you and you will not be going home—this will be your new home. You can have some things of yours brought from home; it will be quiet; you will not suffer. You are in luck; we have an open bed so this can happen soon."

We were stunned and in shock—I have no words to describe how I felt.

Our doctor on the unit overturned the decision to move our boy. She told him, "You can stay here with us." This was impactful because our son was blind and, on a ventilator, so he was anxious about not being able to breathe. The chaotic energy of the ICU was comforting to him, and she understood this.

Our son did stay there, and passed away mid-January. Our doctor came to his celebration, but the most important part of this story is that she wrote my husband and I a letter that said, "Doctors put up walls to protect themselves from painful experiences with their patients. The experience with your son broke through that wall and I'm glad he did. It changed me as a person and I'm going to be a way better doctor because of it."

Both doctors were tasked with virtually the same job. Our doctor from the intensive care unit was guided by the presence of a compassionate space between herself and her patient, allowing for some adjustment to protocol. Most importantly, there was connection and relationship that created the feeling of being valued, being seen, even in an extraordinary circumstance.

The doctor tasked with facilitating end-of-life was guided by process and procedure, and established a patient-centred relationship that supported the best interest of her patient. It was truthful, authentic, and supportive. However, it was not demonstrative of a sincere, human-to-human connection. It was not demonstrative of a relationship that reflected feelings of being valued, being seen, being cared about. Imagine that same scenario in a classroom. Educators often hide behind the processes and procedures aligned with accepted and established student-centred protocols. They often fail to attend to the human, emotional, unique needs of the student.

Which one would you choose to be?

As educators we see hundreds of children. Some of those children will challenge our abilities of knowing how to reach and teach them, some will challenge our abilities to manage their complex behaviors, some may just plain scare us. When we meet these children, we will face difficult decisions, and some decisions may lead us to choose an educational setting outside of the one we are providing. What is important is that you create an experience for the student in which they feel and know that you see their essence, not just their circumstance. As an example, my friend and colleague Steve Cairns shared this story with me: "This reminds me of a protected class that we had in our school; one of the students would fall into the scary category. This teacher met every student with a hug at the door of the classroom and for this most challenging student she would whisper that she had more hugs for him than he could ever need. Soon other classroom teachers changed from fear to care for this student."

Regarding my story earlier with the little girl coming to my classroom, I was the facilitator of Grade 3 programming, and I failed to see her. The message I sent was "You don't belong in my class with your peers." Knowing what I know today, the message I should have sent and now wish I had sent is, "What do I need in order to be able to support you? Come on in and we will figure this out."

Consider how you show up for others. What is the story in your head that is reinforcing your beliefs or truths about diversity? **Know that it is not simply about what you *DO*; what is critical is to know what you must *BE*.**

The inclusion call to action is asking you to challenge those beliefs and consider other opportunities and possibilities. Be curious about what inclusive practice really means. Ask what you need to understand, what you need to believe in order to provide you with the confidence to shift your practice. In other words, belief initiates a search for knowledge that will allow us to do what is right for all children.

Chapter Three

HOW TO GET TO BEING

People do not normally see the connection between their beliefs, their thoughts, and their experiences. Beliefs are invisible and hard to detect, but you can discover them by paying attention to your thoughts, listening to yourself talk, and observing your own actions. Mike Dooley teaches that if you change what you think, say, and do, you will gradually change your lived experiences— and that will begin to change your belief system, revising your "Book of Law."

The work of understanding our personal beliefs can be emotional. According to Mike Dooley, emotions are a gift because they provide valuable feedback on our progress through life. He says that good or pleasant emotions signal confirmation and encouragement that we are on the right path. Unpleasant or uncomfortable emotions can signal the need for a necessary course change and an opportunity to reconsider our perspective on a particular situation or experience. Consider that our beliefs come first, shape our perceptions, and then create our emotions.

In chapter 1, I talked about my experience of receiving a student with significant needs early in my teaching career. At that time, I believed that being a good teacher was evidenced by my level of confidence in knowing what to do. When I first met the little girl, I had a very strong emotional reaction that created fear, anxiety, and powerlessness: I knew that I did not know what to do.

My perception of the situation was that I should not be her teacher because a teacher that was trained would support and serve her successfully. Working with Mike Dooley, taught me that the strong emotions I had in this situation were providing a signal to me of a limiting belief I held and this limiting belief was preventing me from becoming my best self. If I knew then what I have come to know now I would have challenged that belief and opened myself up to looking at opportunities and possibilities of this new learning experience and as a result welcomed the little girl into my class with a new belief that we would work it out together.

Now when an uncomfortable or unpleasant emotion surfaces during a particular experience, I notice my thoughts and what I am perceiving about that situation and become curious about the underlying belief or truth that I hold about that experience. If I take the time to slow down and walk myself through this process it amazes me of how often I can identify limiting beliefs or truths that I hold that do not serve me.

Facing adverse situations generally creates unpleasant or uncomfortable emotions and at some point, in our lives, most of us will encounter adverse experiences. These occurrences likely interrupt our comfortable and safe daily routines and can be unpleasant and painful. Teachers are now reporting that classrooms are becoming more diverse, and express concern about the degree of complexity associated with diverse needs. Noticeably, these identified concerns focus on those aspects of the situation that challenge an existing identity or belief system about teaching practice. Limiting beliefs within teaching show up when pedagogical practices and beliefs do not adjust or align with an environment that appears to be changing. Many teachers continue to teach the way they have always taught, and hold the same expectations and identity about their teaching that they have always held. **I know I did.**

So, what changed for me?

I have written a book called *Could This Be Grace?* that is a powerful story about my personal journey through multiple adverse experiences created by raising two boys who, in their early thirties, succumbed to a devastating rare genetic disease. In my book I describe many of my experiences as painful, crushing, breath-stealing moments that had a huge impact on my life and the lives of my family members. This journey taught me about the impact and experience of adversity and loss, but also about the wonderful insights on how to feel resilient and hang onto hope during troubled times. I learned to ask the right questions and to focus on the things that I was meant to focus on, as Mike Dooley teaches. The lessons I learned because of my situation have had a positive impact on my life.

> *"Our strength grows out of our weakness. Not until we are pricked and stung and sorely shot at, awakens the indignation which arms itself with secret forces."[9] Ralph Waldo Emerson*
>
> *Difficult circumstances can impel you on an inward journey that deepens your conscious connection with your essential self. They also open your eyes to a greater purpose in life, enhance your compassionate connection with others, and enable you to be of greater service to the world.[10]*
>
> *"For everything you have missed, you have gained something else."[11] Ralph Waldo Emerson*

One of the lessons I learned was to know myself, and I learned about myself by asking: who was I, what were my beliefs, my thoughts, my way of being in the world. For example, at the time, as a parent and teacher I held a belief that to be good in both those roles I needed to know what to do.

---

[9] Ronald Hulnick, Mary Hulnick, *Loyalty to Your Soul: The Heart of Spiritual Psychology*, (Hay House, Inc., 2010) pg. 119

[10] Ronald Hulnick, Mary Hulnick, *Loyalty to Your Soul: The Heart of Spiritual Psychology*, (Hay House, Inc., 2010 pg. 119

[11] Ronald Hulnick, Mary Hulnick, *Loyalty to Your Soul: The Heart of Spiritual Psychology*, (Hay House, Inc., 2010) pg. 119

As a mom, because I did not have the experience, background, or training to parent a blind child (and therefore did not know what to do) I went back to graduate school to learn more and to know more so that I **would** know what to do. I convinced myself that if I developed a program to teach blind children the skills to function as a sighted person, folks would not know they were blind. This was my belief about being a "good mom."

I shared earlier that as a Grade 3 teacher, when a student arrived at my class with profound needs, I was thinking she did not belong in my class, because I taught Grade 3 and I didn't know how to teach a child that did not already possess many of the prerequisite skills I expected a Grade 3 student to possess.

Notice that the agreements I made early on in my life became my subconscious belief system, which governed my interpretation of the world. I believed that to be good or successful at something, I needed to know what to do. Also, I had a belief that having a disability such as blindness would interfere with quality of life. I believed that my son needed to learn skills that would support him in showing up in the world just like a sighted person. High expectations for my son were possible only if he had the skills to be in the world in the same way a sighted person would. This belief system certainly was not in the best interest of my son or my students. It was a limiting belief that was getting in the way and preventing me from becoming my best self.

One day my son, Ben, asked me why I was so worried about him not playing soccer with the other kids, and he told me he was happy doing what he was doing. He went on to ask me why I thought that it would be a good idea for him to be out in that field in the first place.

Another day he asked me, if there was an operation available that would restore his vision, would I want him to have the operation? Well, I immediately felt conflicted. If I told him I would want the operation, I was worried he would hear a message that I did not accept him as he was—a dilemma for sure, a trap maybe? Instead of providing an answer, I gave the question back to him and said, "I think that is an important decision for you to make, not me. What would you decide?" He responded almost immediately, "I won't want the operation because reading print would be hard and so then I wouldn't be able to read." I realized immediately his pride in the fact that he was recognized as an accomplished Braille reader, and he loved to read, it was his gift. I was so thankful that I took the time and created the space for him to be seen by me.

The human condition begs to be seen, to be heard, and to have a sense of contribution. When "thyself" is known, one can be totally present to others and come alongside them on their life's journey. When I was born, our family lived in the same town as my grandmother, which meant I saw her often. At the time I started school we had to move away, because my dad got a job in the city. I missed my grandmother and always looked forward to the times when we could visit. I remember that she always read to me, sat, and had tea with me, and listened to all my stories. She pointed out those things that she saw as my strengths and told me someday I was going to be a great teacher. My grandmother really made me feel seen. She made me feel that I mattered and that I had a contribution to make. My grandmother knew how to *be present* for me, and invested the time to show up in a way that empowered me to believe in myself.

What I have learned is that when a compassionate space is created to *see* the other you can feel the transformative spirit of the relationship. It feels amazing, like jumping up into the clouds with joy.

The experience with our boys changed our family path and we found ourselves on a new journey—a journey full of adversity, which invited disability to become a part of our identity and included many, many unexpected experiences. We travelled with sick kids and over the years the boys were hospitalized hundreds of times. Our son Erik, for example, had a period in his life where he was in hospital for two years. Our family was involved with twenty to twenty-five different specialists, and we had a revolving door in our home. Often, I would arrive at work after a night when I had not been to bed and I was exhausted. On one of these days a teammate came into my office and sat. She just looked at me and seemed to be a little agitated. When I asked her what was wrong, she burst out, "I just don't know what to do for you!"

She was so sincere and so obviously very concerned. She wanted to help, she wanted to comfort me in my pain. At that moment, what popped into my head were the words, "You don't have to do anything, but it feels really good that you are here with me; you just have to be." What was happening in our family with our boys felt so isolating, and here she was standing witness to my pain, and I did not feel so all alone.

It is not as much about what you DO—it is critically important about how you ARE.

Living in your head allows you to put up walls to your emotions. There are rules, protocols, and logic (we think). We deal with facts, there is no judgement or opinion. The story is academically sound, and it feels safe. When we allow ourselves to pay attention to our heart, we notice the feelings and the emotions that live there. These emotions are connected to our beliefs, morals, and ethics. There can be a sense of spiritual connectedness, hope, wonder, dreams, and imagination.

In the face of adversity or trauma we need both the head and the heart, but sometimes the immenseness of the experience feels too difficult or painful to manage and we learn to put up walls and intentionally avoid the feelings. So, when my colleague experienced me in emotional pain, her instinct told her to "do something" to help make it a little less painful. In the moment, when it is not obvious what you could or should do, you say, "I don't know what to do for you," or "let me know if there is something I can do," —just like my colleague did.

Doing is a head thing, and it is just that—a thing, like a meal, flowers, or a gift. In the absence of the heart, the pain is not acknowledged or seen and the experience can be extremely isolating. When I looked around, I noticed that life was going on for those around me, but I felt like my life was on hold. When I told my colleague that she just needed to *be*, it became a heart experience, and that is what I needed—connection. To hear a friend or colleague say, "I'm here, I'm not going anywhere, I'll sit with you," creates the experience of feeling seen and having your pain validated. I noticed my emotions shifted from despair to a feeling of comfort.

The experience with my friend and colleague was one of many that moved me along my journey to better understand *being*. My relationship with adversity and diversity was changing. I was less intimidated when facing the reality that I did not know what to do, and gave myself permission to be vulnerable, curious, and inviting. That got me thinking that inclusive practice is as much about how we show up—how we *are*—as it is about how we *do*. It is a belief about how you view diversity, which is reflected in your decisions and behaviors when faced with it.

Knowing yourself, by integrating the head and the heart as well as understanding your belief system and identifying those limiting beliefs that are not serving you, is important work.

Equally important to knowing oneself is knowing one another. Relationships and connections are vital to the human condition, and for our relationships and connections to be successful, we must take the time **to know the other**.

So, ask yourself, what might have happened to this student or individual that caused them to show up the way they do—are they hungry, are their needs being met, have they been treated well, do they feel loved and safe? Be curious about their back story.

I watched a powerful video[12] about a boy arriving late to class every morning. The teacher's style was very structured and demanded that students follow all instructions and protocols that were in place. One of these protocols happened to be "You will not be late for class," and this boy had obviously violated that rule. His punishment was to stand at the front of the class, hold his hand out in front of the teacher and receive a slap from the

---

[12] "Teacher Punishes Kid for Being Late to School, Then He Finds the Truth," Klipland.com, accessed March 29, 2023, *https://klipland.com/video/ teacher-punishes-kid-for-being-late-to-school-then-he-finds-the-truth.*

teacher's ruler. This scenario continued for many days; the boy arrived late, he put out his hand, received the slap, returned to his desk, and the teacher continued with the lesson. One day, as the teacher was on his way to school, he spotted the boy wheeling a loved one in a wheelchair from his home to a caregiver. The boy was hurrying and the teacher realized that this boy had a responsibility to fulfill each morning, and this was the reason he arrived late. The boy accepted that he had violated the teacher's rule and each day took his punishment. After learning the boy's story, the teacher reacted differently when the boy arrived late at school. Rather than have the boy put out his hand for the punishment, the teacher offered the ruler to the boy and put his own hand out to receive the punishment.

The teacher's lesson in this story was about the boy's back story; Instead of creating a compassionate space between himself and the boy and looking for an understanding or meaning for the boy's continued violation of the rule, he assumed, and in the absence of information continued to punish the boy. Rather than offer his hand for punishment, I believe a more acceptable response would have been for the teacher to welcome the boy with a warm smile and later acknowledge the boy's situation and offer praise for his care and attention to his family.

Getting to know myself and taking the time to create a **compassionate space** between myself and others, allowed me to get to know and understand others and really helped me face the degree of adversity that confronted us.

When I got out of my head and started to pay closer attention to those around me, especially my son, great things began to happen. An important question that has guided me in this work is, "What is the experience of an individual in the presence of me? How is my presence making them feel?"

My doctoral research from years ago was a qualitative study on the school experience of successful blind adults. The participants of my study were nominated to the study based on established criteria that identified them as "successful adults." As an educator and mother of a totally blind child, I was curious about those factors within their educational experience that may have contributed to their success as adults. My hope was that the insights I gained from the study could then be replicated within educational environments, in order to benefit all children.

The experience of this research influenced me not only as a professional but as a human being. It provided me with the opportunity to put into practice the things I learned about the importance of understanding the experience of an individual in the presence of me.

I thought about how the development of our belief system applied to my study. Consider life as a stage stretched out before individuals; ahead of us are expectations of life. As we travel across the stage, those expectations are confirmed and our belief systems begin to take hold. Passage across a stage that is flat may feel comfortable and, in most cases, manageable. Therefore, we continue to move across day by day, learning, growing, and playing out our lives.

Along the way, we may meet challenges or problems that offset the balance of this stage. The nature and intensity of the challenge will vary from situation to situation and individual to individual. The more severe the influence of the challenge, the greater the tilt of the stage. An upward tilt of the stage may make the journey feel temporarily interrupted until the problem is resolved, so that the stage rebalances itself, allowing individuals to feel that they can continue. A journey that is interrupted or made difficult may need positive influences to rebalance the stage.

A colleague of mine reported that as educators, we need to understand each learner's degree of achievement. Any student learning a new skill or concept may be challenged more than their peers. Consider that the acquisition of skill for one child could be like skating on a rink that has a tilt, while others glide around the rink with ease and the opportunity to practice the addition of the new skill or concept. Be mindful also, of the fact that for some learners' acquisition of a skill is too easy, and therefore there could be a risk of them becoming bored.

Diversity may impose challenges not only for individuals with diverse needs, but for those individuals around them. The participants in my study described their school experiences by identifying polarizing factors—the challenges of blindness—and the positive influencing factors. One of the important themes from my research that speaks to knowing the other was the theme of being disconnected versus the need for being connected or seen.

The element of connectedness is one of the primary ingredients for the process of forming an identity. My research participants held a sense of purpose and a place in life. Being disconnected is associated with feelings of loneliness, fear, and helplessness. It is a difficult feeling to make sense of because your physical presence gives you one message and your brain and heart tell you something different. As a mother, I cuddled and comforted my son—providing physical presence—but my heart and brain were looking for ways to help him appear sighted. The message I clearly gave him was that he was not seen.

My participants reported experiences of professionals who were knowledgeable and comfortable with blindness becoming involved with their programming; sometimes, this created situations where teachers and parents were intimidated, and as a result gave up their responsibilities and duties and allowed the professionals to be in control. In these circumstances, the participants had a sense of being disconnected from those closest to them.

Our current educational system exacerbates that disconnect between home and school. The inclusionary process must reach out to parents, family, and community members to create the "safety net" or the "net of belonging," to ensure feelings of significance, belonging, and "being known."

Parents, teachers, and significant others can give the message of disconnectedness in several different ways as well. One of these ways is offering praise for ordinary behaviors. If we praise students with diverse needs for doing ordinary things, we send the message that we believe they are not capable of doing any better. My participants reported that there is a tremendous amount of satisfaction in getting a compliment when you really have worked to achieve something. It is important to work with all students to identify goals and expectations that are realistic, appropriate, and meaningful, and that facilitate that feeling of satisfaction and contribution.

As a mother, I eventually realized that I had created a situation within our family that likely resulted in my daughter feeling disconnected. We were struggling with the challenges we faced with our boys. These struggles were profound in many ways. In the early years we travelled to the hospital in Boston; as I mentioned, we made thirty-one trips. Both boys were hospitalized hundreds of times in many different hospitals, and as they got older sometimes those hospitals were not even in our city or province. Our boys were not well, and that meant lots of sleepless nights, lots of anxiety-filled conversations, and many challenges to problem-solve as we attempted to carve out some sort of normal life.

Our eldest child, our daughter, is healthy and vibrant. She was an excellent student and never gave us any reason for concern or worry. She was and still is beautiful and amazing, and I am so grateful for her presence. Nevertheless, I was so caught up in our journey with the boys that I totally took for granted the absolute perfection of my daughter. I assumed everything was all right; she did not ask for any time or attention, and I was not present enough to offer it. Sadly, I did not take the time to *be* for her, to be as connected with her as I was with our sons. I failed to check in with her to find out what her experience of our situation was, or how it was impacting her. I did not ask what she might be worrying about, what fears she was holding on to, or whether she felt seen and heard. I had unintentionally created a situation where she likely felt a loss of connection. I know this because I have watched her struggle in her adult life with the effects of being exposed to a traumatic experience, and we have openly talked about it. It has become a powerful lesson for me of the importance of creating that compassionate space where an individual can really feel seen and heard. Here is an example of how the lessons I was learning impacted my behavior.

Several years ago, I began to write Maren and the boys a Christmas letter. Each year I tried to be creative and wrote these letters based on a theme and my intention and purpose for the letter was to capture the experience I had in their presence. Here is a copy of a letter I wrote to Maren shortly after my grandson was born that expresses my authentic and sincere feelings of "seeing" her.

BUCKET FILL-OSOPHY According to ME

My dearest Maren,

Your dad and I remember with our hearts those tender special moments that you may have forgotten. When you hear us talk about those events of the past it's with the feelings of the present, confirming the enduring nature of our bond. Each and every one of these moments has been filling our buckets from the time you came into our lives. Everyone has an invisible bucket that needs to be filled and these buckets are a vitally important part of the human being. Our buckets are rich and overflowing because of you – you are one amazing BUCKET FILLER!!

Of course, I love every single thing about you and just being with you is rewarding and very special. Somehow though, that just doesn't capture the essence of being with you – it's much bigger than that. You inspire me, and you inspire me in ways that are life changing. You make me feel excited about being me and curious about all those possibilities of "me" that I would never have considered. Your passion and tenacity for the journey towards becoming the "unconditional self that is divine" is infectious and the more time

I spend with you the more committed I become to this journey for myself. That's who you are and I am in awe of your magnificence.

Daily, I peer into my imaginary bucket to embrace and reflect on the gifts that you've been filling my bucket with: "it is what it is", "what's the mirror?" "we have enough", "stand in your power", "how we are being, manifests what gets created", "learn the lesson now or learn the lesson later – the stackers have lots of beer in the cooler", and of course the biggy, "Live with Fierce Integrity (stand in your truth)".

With your ongoing guidance, coaching and loving support I continue to make gains towards living my life with the Fierce Integrity that you have so beautifully and articulately described and modelled in your book. I am enjoying this journey; it's fulfilling and rewarding. I am especially enjoying this journey because I am with you – a treasure and bucket filler.

When you and I talk about the degree of suffering currently in our world I am comforted by the realization that you've got our backs! You wear many hats: leader, spiritual guide- perhaps a new age prophet, bucket filler, coach, mom, wife, sister, daughter, yogi, etc. Regardless of the hat you are wearing, you ignite inspiration in those that you touch because you are an inspiring being.

I love you

My research participants and my daughter have taught me the importance of slowing down and paying close attention to those in my presence. Through them I recognized that I had adopted behaviors that negatively impacted my students with diverse needs, as well as students and others, that did *not* draw my attention. I had allowed a state of disconnect to exist between myself, my daughter, and others as a result of my belief that I was not a good mother and teacher because I did not know what to do, and was relying on other professionals to make decisions. An important point to acknowledge is that a difficult adverse experience consumes a tremendous amount of energy and focus; I found it all-consuming. At the time, I failed to recognize that the significant beings in my network could have been a source of comfort if I had allowed them to be welcomed and valued in my presence. I felt very isolated and alone during this time, and failing to include others contributed to the experience of disconnectedness we all must have been feeling.

I embraced the concept of *being*. To *be* is to feel fulfilled. Experiences of *being* are associated with love, caring, connecting, and commonalities. To *be* means that you are part of a whole, and as a part of the whole you belong and others share that space with you.

My research participants identified positive strategies they experienced that fostered *being*, which made them feel like they belonged. They reported being assigned responsibilities or chores, being chosen for leadership positions, having high expectations and a vision of possibilities, and being encouraged to participate in competitive situations.

Years ago, I was driving home and passed our local church. Posted on their outside sign was the following message: *People may forget what you say, they may forget what you did, but they will never forget how you made them feel.*

I think of this when I ask myself the question, **"What is the experience an individual has in the presence of me?"**

Chapter Four

BEING SETS THE STAGE FOR BELONGING

Being sets the stage for belonging because the decisions we make and the behaviors we exhibit are determined by our personal beliefs. Throughout this chapter, I am reflecting on the important work of researchers and my personal experience to illustrate how our decisions and behaviors promote the feeling of belonging or the feeling of being disconnected.

When I was engaged in my doctoral research, I was curious about how belief systems were developed within individuals and how expectations were established. As a result, I saw the need to review theories of learning and utilized Hergenhahn's work[13] in which he outlines the essential features of the major theories of learning and examines their relationships with educational practices. Through my review of Hergenhahn's work I learned that according to Tolman's theory of learning, belief systems can be changed from experience or knowledge.[14] My belief system was fundamentally changed through experience *and* knowledge.

---

[13] B. R. Hergenhahn, *An Introduction to Theories of Learning*, (NJ: Prentice Hall, 1988)

[14] Dianne McConnell, *School Experiences of Successful Adults with Blindness*, (Doctoral Dissertation. Edmonton: University of Alberta, 1997). pg. 144

As you may have already noted, my experiences were extreme and profound. Knowledge came from self-reflection within the context of brilliant research and insights from experts in the fields of psychology, sociology, and human development. One of the most prominent figures in all three areas is world-renowned developmental clinical psychologist Dr. Gordon Neufeld.

Neufeld's work is primarily based on Dr. John Bowlby's Theory of Attachment. Dr. Gordon Neufeld believes that foundational in education is the establishment of solid and distinctive relationships with children, which he calls attachment-based. He and Dr. Gabor Maté, have written a book called *Hold on to Your Kids: Why Parents Need to Matter More Than Peers*[15] that describes the theory of attachment.

Neufeld explains how a child's healthy relationships with parents, teachers, and significant adults can be guided through the understanding and application of the six stages of attachment:

- **Proximity**: The need to be close, to touch, to be touched, to be nearby, to see you, to hear you, to smell you.
- **Sameness:** the tendency to want to be like the people they love.
- **Belonging** or Loyalty: the feeling or strong sense of acceptance within family and potentially from other key caregivers, such as a teacher.
- **Significance:** the need for a child to feel special or significant to those closest to them.
- **Love**: the need to be loved and to feel that love come through in our actions, in our tone.
- **Being Known**: a strong sense that the key people in a child's life know that child well and have a deep sense of who they truly are.

---

[15] Gordon Neufeld and Gabor Maté, *Hold on to Your Kids: Why Parents Need to Matter More Than Peers,* (Toronto: Vintage Canada, 2004).

Through Dr. Neufeld's work we learn that building a relationship with a child should be our focus and priority. Neufeld identifies how this relationship can be fostered through the child's developmental stages. He says that attachment is the longing for human togetherness because we all seek emotional closeness, intimacy, love, and the need to belong and matter. Schools should become environments that have these teachings embedded within them.

Another source that confirms the importance of belonging comes from the Hasso Plattner Institute of Design, also known as d. school, which was founded at Stanford University in 2004.[16] The purpose of the program is to attract students from all disciplines to learn how the thinking behind design can enrich their work and unlock possibilities and opportunities for innovative practice. In 2022, Susie Wise published *Design for Belonging* as a guide to support individuals in building communities that are inclusive. Her view, which is supported in the research, is that belonging is foundational within the design of these communities. It is the thing that matters most. She says, ". . . having a sense of belonging leads to flourishing in every environment and group, big and small, from your home to the culture at large." [17] Susie identifies three essential elements in the work of designing for belonging:

- feeling of belonging
- seeing of belonging
- shaping of belonging

Feeling of Belonging

I believe the best way to understand belonging is to recognize the feelings that are created through the experience of belonging. Words like comfortable, invited, validated, seen, or heard are

---

[16] *https://dschool.stanford.edu/how-to-start-a-dschool/*
[17] Susie Wise, *Design for Belonging: How to Build Inclusion and Collaboration in Your Communities,* (Emeryville, CA: Ten Speed Press, 2022), xiii.

used when individuals describe an environment or experience where they belonged.

According to the research participants of my doctoral studies, the most rewarding situations for them were those where they were accepted on the same level as everyone else and therefore genuinely included. For example, here is a quote from one of my co-researchers, "I suppose I would like to just have been considered the equal of every student in the classroom. The groups I am most **comfortable** with are the ones with people in the room that do not see me as anything special,"

In these situations, the individuals around them believed in them and expected that they would contribute equally to the group. They respected high standards, enjoyed the thrill of competition, and praised those who pushed them. As my co-researchers reflected on their school experiences, it became obvious that being **invited and validated** were vital in supporting their feelings of being one of the groups.

My husband and I travelled to many cities for medical treatments for our boys and we met doctors who failed to acknowledge our isolation, which was created by distance and lack of support. They were expert in their professional skills, but we felt disconnected. This experience caused me to reflect on my role as a teacher and I wondered how many times I failed to recognize that I likely had many students and their families over the years that were new to the community, or were in a situation or circumstance in their lives where they felt they did not have support. At the time, if I had recognized the importance of creating the feelings of belonging, I may have considered inviting the family to an informal meet-and-greet, sending home a welcome and information package, or sending a message that the student and their family had become an important part of our school community. When we met Dr. Walton, in Boston, he **validated** our isolation and we began to understand belonging. I needed to do the same thing for my students and their families.

I was intrigued as I read *Design for Belonging* to discover the word *othering*. According to Susie Wise, *othering* is the opposite of belonging; it describes how people from a different group from one's own are treated, and it generally depicts negativity or inferiority. Susie Wise says that othering and belonging show up everywhere and once you understand the difference between the two and are familiar with the terms, they become very visible to you, the observer.

When Ben was in elementary school it became obvious how important being invited to the birthday party of a schoolmate was for the students, and of course their moms. Ben received the coveted invitation to the party and was thrilled to go. I dropped him at the party and moms were asked to return in a couple of hours for pickup. When I returned to the party, a few minutes before the scheduled time, I observed the children running and playing together out in the yard and Ben standing off to the side, alone. He had not been incorporated into the game and was obviously treated as if he was not there. I do not believe this was intentional rather, it was the result of a lack of awareness about how to revise the game to provide the accessibility for him to participate. In failing to recognize his needs, the experience created for him was that of *othering*. He felt like he did not belong, was not accepted and was inferior to his peers.

Examples of *othering* include not being waited on when entering a café, not seeing your group represented at a community event, being cut off in a conversation, not being asked for your opinion when all the others in the group were polled, and not being selected as part of a team or group within the school. These may seem like small or one-time occurrences, but the initial experience and hurt of the moment is there, and it is therefore important that we understand and acknowledge where and when *othering* might be occurring. Remember, *inclusion* is the opposite of *othering* and clearly requires an intentional awareness or knowing, along with belief and action. *Othering* seems to me to be a social default, and the best way to create inclusion is to teach and model inclusion.

Victor Cary, senior director with the National Equity Project in Oakland, California, says that people casually speak about a "sense of belonging." He insists that it is a sense because you feel belonging and othering in your body.[18] As school systems embrace the concept of transformation towards designing educational environments and programs that are inclusive, creating *belonging* should be a primary goal. *Belonging* can be sensed by the feelings generated, and a school system can easily collect this information by first developing relationships within their staff, families, and community, and then surveying them on how they are feeling as members of the school community. To ensure that one fully understands what is being seen and felt with regards to what is happening in the system, they must be fully participating.

Seeing of Belonging

I have just explored the concept of how *belonging* and *othering* feels, and how those feelings have been created by experiences we have had in our lives. Susie Wise explains that we can construct or design experiences that create a sense of belonging if we understand the pieces of the journey. These pieces include **invitation, entering, participating, code-switching, contributing, flowing, dissenting, repairing, diverging, and exiting.**[19]

An **invitation** to an event or experience should consider what you want the individual to feel when they receive it. When Ben was in elementary school, an important event for him and his peers was being invited to a classmate's birthday party. The families of the students in Ben's class were aware of the importance of receiving the coveted birthday invitation and intentionally thought about the importance of connecting with him directly to extend the invite. They connected with Ben through the telephone, which made Ben feel like an important member of the class. The fact that families recognized that Ben would not see a printed invitation and wanted him to feel included is an example of how important an invite is in creating the feeling of belonging.

---

[18] Susie Wise, *Design for Belonging: how to build inclusion and collaboration in your communities,* (Emeryville, CA: Ten Speed Press, 2022) pg.7

[19] Susie Wise, *Design for Belonging: how to build inclusion and collaboration in your communities,* (Emeryville, CA: Ten Speed Press, 2022) pg.32,33

When I was working for Alberta Education, leading a project focusing on the future of special education in the province, we invited community members to participate in a public engagement event to provide them with the opportunity to express their views on the topic. Our intention was to create an experience for the community members where they felt validated, and had a sense that we cared about their views with respect to this topic. What we had not considered was whether our materials were accessible to everyone that wanted to participate; for example, ensuring barrier-free venues or materials offered in a variety of formats (Braille, large print, audio, translators, and additional languages). Neglecting to ensure that our sessions were accessible to everyone participating created a sense of *othering* rather than *belonging*.

According to Susie Wise, important questions to consider when making an invitation include:

- Who does it come from?
- How findable is it?
- Does it require prior knowledge to understand?
- Does it require specific technologies to view?
- Is access restricted in any way?

The second element of the belonging journey is **entering** a space or group; it sets the stage for **participation**. Most of us have been invited to join a group or some sort of social gathering, whether at a conference, a wedding reception, a house party, a gathering of friends and so on. I have noticed that some individuals are very comfortable and relaxed entering these spaces, but I have always had a sense of apprehension and anxiety. What I have noticed is my comfort with entering the space depends on how the space is designed. If the space provides me with the opportunity to easily join with some individuals upon entering, my social anxiety relaxes. Or, if the room is designed so that finding a place or understanding how to participate is easy, I find it more comfortable to enter. When you are inviting individuals to join you, consider how you design the space to provide participants with the necessary cues for how to belong.

Participation may be a difficult concept to understand. The ways in which participation occurs can vary from individual to individual, and the experience may look very different. The degree to which one participates may vary, but the important thing to consider is that individuals at the event feel like they are present and are meant to be there. Planning an event and taking into consideration options for participation requires attention to many details. Previously, I talked about the public engagement work I was involved with at Alberta Education. Our intention was to facilitate an event that provided the opportunity for everyone to participate. To achieve this goal, we had to do a lot of planning. We researched the communities where the events were taking place to learn about who lived in the community, and tried to anticipate barriers that might prevent full participation, then made decisions to minimize or remove those barriers. We learned from our mistakes and attempted to correct them at upcoming events, and we noticed how our attention to details facilitated participation.

Code-switching is a term that describes situations where an individual will communicate in a certain way with one group, and then change their mode of communication when participating in another group. A simple example is a teenager conversing with their friends and then entering a conversation with their parents. The type of language or vocabulary may change; the intonations, phrasing, and overall means of communicating may sound different in each scenario. I noticed when Ben was growing up that his friends talked with him in the same way they talked with each other; but often, in an adult setting the adults would talk to him more slowly and much more loudly than when talking with others. Ben would feel annoyed and would remind them that he could hear just fine, it was his vision that was a problem. This example points out that code-switching can foster *othering* if we do not understand it. On the other hand, it can be a powerful resource and an excellent strategy to foster belonging. Code-switching is about listening, and is an authentic part of communication.

Contributing can take many forms but ultimately it is the comfort and ability to be yourself and to show up in an environment and feeling the freedom to express yourself through words or actions. Saying something, bringing something, caring for other participants, or simply showing up are all ways in which contribution can be felt and expressed. The design of *contribution* within an environment fostering belonging has two aspects: what the individual is contributing and how the contribution is received. When I was in Grade 6, a requirement for Grade 6 students in my school was to participate in the school choir. I loved to sing and was thrilled to be a member of this group. One day during lunchtime practice, the choir director stopped us in the middle of a number and pointed at me and told me to sing. I was scared, but did as I was asked and started to sing the song we were singing. After several notes I was told to stop and the choir director pointed to the door and told me to leave. I was kicked out of the choir. That experience was a very long time ago but the feeling of not being able to sing remains strong within me today. *Contribution* is an important element of *belonging*, especially if individuals can contribute from their areas of strength. Sharing our strengths and gifts with others has an important ripple effect within the community, and fosters belonging.

Flow is a term used to describe the coming together of a group; some say the group has "gelled." Flow exemplifies a natural connection, of one activity or aspect of an activity moving smoothly to another. Roles of individuals participating in the group express their contributions in a seamless, fluid way. Groups working with flow express a sense of feeling good and successful. Many recount that participating was a great experience. Susie Wise expressed that signs of flow may include the hum of chitchat while working, laughter, and the ability to accomplish goals without stress.

It is not reasonable to imagine that a group exists in absence of **dissenting** views. What is important is how the group manages or responds to those differences. If the expression of individual differences is encouraged, allowed, and welcomed, one assumes that the individuals feel safe and secure within the group. According to John Powell, Director of the Othering and Belonging Institute at the University of California, Berkeley, ". . . belonging means more than just being seen. Belonging entails having a meaningful voice and the opportunity to participate in the design of social and cultural structures. Belonging means having the right to contribute and make demands on society and political institutions." [20]

I was really looking forward to registering Ben in playschool as soon as he was old enough. When the time arrived, the phone call was very engaging and I was assured that Ben would be a welcome addition to the program. Several days later, I received a return call from a member of the registration committee. Apparently, someone had contacted them and informed them that Ben was blind, and accepting him into the program would take too much of the teacher's time and other children would suffer; therefore, he should not be accepted. The call was to inform me that they had rejected his registration. I was shocked and hurt. I challenged their logic, which resulted in a very awkward and uncomfortable conversation. The result was that the president invited my husband Roy and I to attend a public parent meeting to discuss the pros and cons of Ben's participation in the program. I was nervous to attend the meeting, but thought it was a good opportunity to discuss the benefits and bust the myths of having Ben in the program. When we arrived at the meeting, I noticed little white slips of paper on every chair and wondered about their purpose. As soon as the meeting started, I sensed extreme discomfort from the president as she attempted to explain the situation regarding our intention of registering Ben in the program.

---

[20] Wise, *Design for Belonging*, pg., 64.

Without any thought of facilitating a conversation or inviting Roy or I to offer some teachings, she informed the group that we were going to vote and asked for hands up to those who voted in favor of having Ben in the program, and subsequently hands up for those opposed. WOW—to this day, we remember the small number that voted against his participation and are grateful for those that voted in favor, as he had an amazing experience alongside his peers in playschool.

A group without a trusted and accepted process for managing dissension risks othering, and therefore lack of cohesion within the group.

We all make mistakes. In education we say that if we do not make mistakes we are not learning. We have worked intentionally in education to encourage taking risks, making mistakes, trying again, and learning our way forward. Behaviors of *othering* can be ingrained in us through generations. In the chapter on *being*, I referenced Don Miguel's work on making an agreement early in life that becomes our truth and then our belief. Our beliefs influence our decisions and behaviors, and as a result we may not initially be aware that we *other* groups of individuals, certain behaviors, traits, or attributes. Becoming aware of those underlying beliefs aids us in challenging those beliefs and in accepting new truths. In situations where we have hurt another as a result of our decisions or behaviors, we can **repair**. Repairing can look very different depending on the circumstance. It could be as simple as a phone call to a friend or family member, or it could mean actively becoming involved in a reconciliation initiative. ***Repairing*** means acknowledging the decision or behavior that caused hurt, taking responsibility by owning it and holding yourself accountable to make the changes you may need to make. Willingness to become vulnerable and make efforts to repair is important and essential to fostering belonging.

We flow in and out of situations, environments, groups, lived experiences, and people's lives in the same way that others flow in and out of our life. Suzie Wise refers to this as **diverging and exiting**. It is the natural way of being. Mark Salinas at the National

Equity Project calls this the "comings and goings,"[21] a way to give voice to schedule modifications that are part of any gathering.

When I began to realize the impact of our situation fostered a feeling of being disconnected in my daughter, I invited her to attend a Louise Hay conference with me, where we had the opportunity to listen to the inspirational speaker Wayne Dyer. During his session he made the comment, "Our children are here to come through us, not to be here for us." I got a nudge in my side from my daughter, with her comment, "Did you hear that?" On reflection, I learned that my feeling of belonging as a family meant that family members were there for me, perhaps fair to say focused on me. I believed this would be expressed by wanting to be with me, agreeing with me, and catering to my needs. At the time, I did not understand that this was a shortcoming on my part; my sense of belonging could not be defined by them providing it for me. I had to find it in myself, and in doing so free them to express themselves, make choices for themselves, and flow beautifully in and out of my life. Giving my daughter permission to become her best self was very powerful in connecting us.

Brené Brown's quote expresses this thought much more clearly, "True belonging is the spiritual practice of believing in and belonging to yourself so deeply that you can share your most authentic self with the world and find sacredness in both being a part of something and standing alone in the wilderness."[22]

I am understanding this concept more and more each day, and find peace and comfort in the ebb and flow of individuals in my life. Friends and family have opportunities and obligations that require them to move away, colleagues come late to a scheduled meeting, participants register for an event and then do not show up. The essence of belonging shows up when we do not judge or take these comings and goings personally. We make room in our expectations about an event, circumstance, or life situation for

---

[21] Wise, *Design for Belonging,* pg.,75.
[22] Wise, *Design for Belonging,* pg., 67.

individuals to be late, present, or absent. True belonging means that when they do arrive, they are authentically welcomed.

Shaping of Belonging

According to Susie Wise, if you want to design or shape a space for belonging you can use what she calls *levers of design*. By definition, a lever is a device that makes moving a force or weight easier, and she outlines the following examples of levers in her book: space, roles, events, rituals, grouping, communication, clothing, food, schedules, and rhythm.

Susie talks about each one of these levers in detail and provides good examples of how one could incorporate them into an environment that supports belonging. She emphasizes the importance of and value of levers being used to set the context for the feeling of belonging to occur. As you begin the process of designing a space for a particular group, consider the outcome rather than outputs and think about the levers you might use to create the overall experience you want your group to have.

As an educational leader, my role was to ensure that our division removed barriers to learning and improved environments for each of our students. I knew that our success depended on our ability to understand the needs of our students. We needed to know their backstories, their hopes and dreams, their passions, and their strengths. We needed to be able to look at each one of our students and say, "*I see you*; I see you, and you are enough just the way you are." In the wisdom of Brené Brown, we wanted students to belong and not just fit in. Embracing diversity meant that we saw it as a strength that enriched us and helped us grow as individuals and educational leaders. As a result, we were more able to design programs and environments where students were happy, healthy, and successful, and received the right supports and services so that they could achieve the outcomes from the programs of study.

In our division our teachers used a variety of levers to help them *see* their students. In kindergarten to Grade 9 we used a classroom profile tool where teachers identified the degree to which students are engaged in different aspects of education, for example literacy, numeracy, transitions, physical literacy, etc. Some teachers sent home interview questions for parents with questions like: "Are there holidays you don't celebrate, and how would you like me to address these in the classroom?" Teachers used academic assessments as well as student-interest inventories to get to know their students. Some even went to their students' community sports games. One school used a "fish out of water" activity to identify students in their school who they believed were not connected to at least two adults in the school. Then, every staff member took on one or two of those students and made it their mission to really get to know and build a connection with them throughout the school year. Building relationships is important to us, and we continually look for additional ways to get to know students in more ways than just academics.

In Shelley Moore's video, *Transforming Inclusive Education*[23], she helps us to see that when we design learning for those students on the edges of our classroom, for our students with the most unique and sometimes challenging needs, then we are more likely to make learning accessible for all our students. In this process, we are truly designing an inclusive environment. In her TEDx Talk "Under the Table,"[24] Moore also talks about the importance of presuming competence for all our learners. Sometimes, we make assumptions about what students can and cannot do and these assumptions can and will influence the design of our learning environments. When we presume competence and believe in our hearts that there are different ways of knowing and different ways of demonstrating learning, then we are open to all the possibilities available to us and our students. When we lean in, when we get curious and walk beside our students to get to know them in deep and authentic ways, we *see* them and embrace them for all that

---

[23] Shelley Moore, "Transforming Inclusive Education," April 4, 2016, presentation, 3:08, *https://www.youtube.com/watch?v=RYtUlU8MjlY*.

[24] Shelley Moore, "Under the Table: The Importance of Presuming Competence," March 11, 2016, presentation, 15:11, *https://www.youtube. com/watch?v=AGptAXTV7m0*.

they are and, thereby, will be better able to identify what specific supports and services our students may need.

Walking into many classrooms, you will notice the efforts made to reduce learning barriers, and there is evidence of student voice and choice. We see teachers working with students to help them identify when they are dysregulated—individuals unable to control their emotions in the same way that others can—and what strategies might work to help them regulate. There are a variety of seating and grouping options from which students can choose, including stand-up desks, couches, wiggle seats, rockers, and bouncy balls. There are fidget toys, quiet spaces, weighted blankets, noise-cancelling headsets, individual spaces, and group spaces. Students are learning to advocate for themselves regarding what they need to help them learn throughout the day. Teachers and students are co-creating clear criteria about what success looks like when student outcomes are met. Learning is accessible because students have access to technology. These technology tools help to personalize learning for many students. What works for one student may not work for another, so as teachers get to know their students, they are improving not only their learning environments but also the design for belonging for all their students.

Chapter Five

WHAT'S GETTING IN THE WAY?

Implementing an education system that is inclusive requires thought and discussion about systemic change—a paradigm shift, an aligned educational response to a student demographic that has become widely diverse. Most people agree with the concept that inclusive environments should be places where thinking and acting demonstrates universal acceptance and promotion of belonging for all learners. I have had the opportunity to be involved with the inclusion conversation for many years, and we are still having the conversation. It feels like most agree philosophically with this concept so I have asked myself: What's getting in the way of making inclusive practice the norm?

When I was the project lead for "Setting the Direction," a framework outlining a vision for an inclusive education system emerged and was approved by government. Under the leadership of then-Minister of Education, the Honorable David Hancock, implementation of this framework demanded systemic change and educational reform to *redesign the educational system as one system for all students.*

We learned that there are two foundational issues that hold teacher's hostage and clinging to less-inclusive pedagogical practices. The first one has to do with individual perspectives and a reluctance to make a critical analysis of one's pedagogical practices, and the second has to do with educational transformation and reform.

I had the opportunity to address Alberta communities following the approval of the framework that had been co-designed with Albertans. My presentation outlined seven examples of the kinds of systemic changes required to transform the education system to be inclusive. To fully implement an education system that is inclusive, the vision of environments where all students experience belonging must be owned at every level of leadership within the system. The culture of any organization is determined by the decisions and behaviors of those in leadership positions.

We celebrated the government acceptance of the framework at a Minister's Forum. Here is a synopsis of the presentation that I delivered in 2010:

Do you Believe?
Reflections of Setting the Direction

We have a dual system of education—one being the regular or general education system and the other the special education system. The two systems operate side by side, each with their own students, teachers, supervisory staff, and funding system.

The collective advice gleaned from the consultation process was that the education system should be one system with a philosophy that takes responsibility for ALL students, including students with special education needs, so that they may truly belong as fully participating and engaged members of the education system. Participants said that if we continue to identify students as "special education students," they will continue to belong to that world and you will continue to perceive that a dual system with separate approaches is in place.

One education system for all is based on four conditions:

- *each student has the right to belong and should be welcomed as full members within the system;*
- *each student has the right to grow and develop in relationships with peers who have diverse skills;*
- *school communities should value diversity, and model inclusive societies;*
- *the education system must be designed to meet the needs, hopes and dreams of each unique student.*
- *Not everyone agrees on the meaning of "inclusion." Some said that inclusion, specifically educational inclusion, describes the process of full integration in a regular or typical classroom—full stop.*

Others expressed concern and fear that the good work and effort that has been done in developing specialized settings, which provide specialized instruction to serve students that cannot—or find it difficult—to learn in a typical or regular classroom environment, would be lost in Setting the Direction. Those who want these specialized learning environments embraced promoted the concept of inclusion as respecting differences by recognizing and valuing programs of choice—the right setting for children at the right time.

And I heard many parents passionately embrace choice. Choice of a faith-based school opportunity, choice of a gender-specific educational environment, choice of a segregated, highly specialized educational environment as examples. People said that inclusion must consider choice, and that a child with special education needs must have the same choices that are available to other children. Inclusion is a powerful word that has many faces, depending on **your** *own personal experience. It feels like the word inclusion has been used in a variety of ways to express what everyone wanted to see and where everyone's thought this vision should be taking us and it is quite clear that not everyone sees it the same way.*

Yet as a result of the work, the journey, the struggle to understand one another and value different points of view, the definition of an inclusive education system that Setting the Direction came up with is:

A way of thinking and acting that demonstrates universal acceptance of, and belonging for, all students. Inclusive education in Alberta means a value-based approach to accepting responsibility for all students. It also means that all students will have equitable opportunity to be included in the typical learning environment or program of choice.

We have been told that this definition is an example of the common ground where everyone's needs can be met. Can this really be an example of what can happen if we believe in one another, trust one another, and collectively work towards a new way of thinking and working in education— to get there, to our new future? Each one of us experiences and interprets the world in our own way—which mean that any one of us sees the world incorrectly.

For me, something very special happened in those Setting the Direction forums. The stories began from perspectives of despair, frustration, and sometimes anger but somehow changed to perspectives that felt hopeful and exciting. The conversations became filled with possibilities and the mood and desire for a different future emerged.

The stories propelled me onwards—beyond bureaucracy, beyond the status quo—to a place where possibilities thrive. I believe those stories have the power to motivate change. Hearing others perspectives provided me with a window that revealed attitudes and beliefs. The stories I heard in every room were real; they represented moments of truth from others worlds and I experienced them as gifts. Each story had the power to influence the others in the room by providing insight into their world and in doing so perhaps changing or affecting attitudes.

The Setting the Direction Framework was presented to the Honorable Dave Hancock, Education Minister, last year. This framework outlines or describes the new future, the THERE, that we are all driving towards. It says that our new future of an inclusive system will have the following attributes:

It is a **system that takes responsibility for ALL students**, and meets the needs of a diverse student population in all school settings.

It is a system that replaces the emphasis on special education "programming" with an **emphasis on achieving outcomes for students**. Getting real and meaningful results—and we do not just mean on tests!

It is a system that develops the comprehensive supports and services **required** to take responsibility for ALL students. A system has a **continuum of support**, which meets the needs of the classrooms, schools, school authorities, and beyond. Because "we're all in this together."

It is a system that takes **an asset-based approach** to meeting the needs of students with special needs and places the emphasis on what students can do, rather than the limitations of their diagnosed condition.

It is a system that respects **data gathered at all levels of the system**, beginning with the family and teacher, and including specialist reports from medical and education experts. It's a system where your voice matters and is taken as seriously as the voice of a therapist or doctor. A system where everyone's knowledge is valued and used meaningfully.

It is a system that recognizes that a successful school journey for all children **begins with quality early learning and care** and concludes with positive high school completion, and acknowledges that smooth transitions throughout the school journey are critical elements of success.

And it is a system that supports students in schools with the services that they need—which may not be exclusively education services, but a range of services that would be delivered collaboratively in the most logical and natural setting, thus "wrapping" services around the student.

Inclusion is a place, a description, and an action. It can look different at different points in time and can represent a continuum of places, supports, and actions. I feel confident that the word INCLUSION is essential to ignite systemic reform. REAL CHANGE. An inclusive system as described above is what I understand to be at the core of the future of education.

Foundational to this work is the need for individuals within the system at every level to change their attitudes. Possibilities open when you believe in something we all need to start believing in ALL kids. We need to respond to this possibility for change by

> *BEING the change and truly believing in all that we are capable of being, knowing, and doing.*
>
> *I think it is fair to say that systemic change begins with every one of us.* **We are the change***. It was Gandhi who said,* **"Be the change you want to see in the world."**

I delivered that presentation thirteen years ago and the messages embedded are consistent with the following messages I am writing today:

1. The education system should adopt a philosophy that takes responsibility for ALL students, including students with special education needs, so that they may truly **belong** as fully participating and engaged members of the education system. Participants said that if we continue to identify students as "special education students," they will continue to belong to that world and you will continue to perceive that a dual system with separate approaches is in place. If we no longer isolate, disconnect, and segregate children, the word inclusion will no longer be necessary.
2. Foundational to this work is the need for individuals within the system at every level to change their attitudes. Changing attitudes **is** possible. Possibilities open when you **believe** in something and I think we all need to start believing in ALL kids. We need to respond to this possibility for change by **BEING.**
3. I think that in this new future, **inclusion is an action.**
4. Inclusion is a powerful word that has many faces, depending on **your** own personal experience. The word inclusion has been used in a variety of ways to express what everyone wanted to see and where everyone thought this vision should be taking us and it is quite clear that not everyone sees it the same way.
5. The word **INCLUSION is essential to ignite systemic reform. REAL CHANGE.**

Inclusion is action and the call is the need for individual and systemic change. We all experience things individually and have our own unique perspectives about the world, and students need to feel seen, heard and experience a sense of belonging.

Personal or individual barriers are created from limiting beliefs, which can show up when we are faced with the challenge of responding to a student with diverse needs.

Earlier I talked about my own experience of a situation where my belief system prevented me from welcoming and accepting a student with complex needs into my classroom. I believed that to be a good teacher I needed to know what to do; in the presence of this student with complex needs, I knew I *did not* know what to do, so I believed that she did not belong with me.

This thinking, which was logical to me at the time, was signaling a limiting belief about my practice, which created a **problem with my practice** in the classroom. As I reflected on this concept of limiting beliefs, I identified several other limiting beliefs I held as a classroom teacher that prevented me from embracing diversity and welcoming all students.

1. I felt that I did not have the capacity to be inclusive in my practice, and I did not have adequate resources.

My student with complex needs did not have the ability to access the material from the way that I was teaching, and I did not know how to make the adjustments in my teaching to reach her. I also believed that the solution to my problem resided in resources outside my classroom that was beyond my ability to access; for example, a specialized classroom or an educational assistant.

2. I felt overwhelmed with the number of other needs in my classroom.

I had the belief that the students in my classroom were a homogeneous group. I knew I had to differentiate slightly, but I believed I would be doing so within the curriculum I was teaching. What I experienced, however, was that many of my students had many needs that I was not expecting; for example, learning disabilities, attention challenges, social-emotional needs, behavior problems and socio-economic challenges. In fact, I think it would be fair to say that there is no such thing as a "typical" student.

3. Pressure regarding human rights and litigation is becoming an increasing concern for jurisdictions.

Our son Ben was blind, and his teachers did not always know or understand the impact his blindness had on his accessing information. For example, one of his teachers in high school did not know how to make an accommodation for him to use a graphic calculator and expected him to do the calculations in his head. As a result, Ben failed the course. At the time, he had applied to attend the World University and was not accepted because of the poor math grade. Some families could easily have interpreted this situation as a human rights complaint. During my experience as a teacher, I occasionally encountered times where the expectations from a family did not align with my capacity to deliver. In those circumstances I found myself in the middle, weighing the rights of one of my students' needs against the rights of the other students in my classroom.

4. Siloed approach to the delivery of services-consultative model versus embedded services.

This concept is clearly aligned with my thinking that the solution to any problem I encountered resided outside of myself— external locus of control. I believed that the right resource, the right service, or support, was the solution I needed to be seeking. Consultants or specialists coming into my classroom, working with an individual student, and leaving me with a list of recommendations that I either did not understand or have time for, left me feeling frustrated or irritated.

5. I was scared!

To be honest, as a teacher I believed I should know what to do and I also believed that everyone expected me to know what to do. I felt alone and scared to admit that I was feeling challenged and overwhelmed.

In summary, the fact is these limiting beliefs were preventing me from believing that I was part of the solution, a valuable member of the team. I had an underlying belief that the solution or strategies for support must come from an "expert." I saw my locus of control as external rather than internal.

Other examples of limiting beliefs could include the following thoughts: I'm too old; I'm not smart enough; I'm not educated enough; I have already tried everything; I don't have the willpower.

Holding onto these limiting beliefs and not recognizing them as such left me feeling overwhelmed, frustrated, and anxious as I experienced the student demographic in my classroom slowly changing. I have heard from colleagues that I wasn't the only one experiencing these feelings. Rather than recognize that these feeling were a result of limiting beliefs, I think many are blaming inclusion for disrupting the system, and this is understandable. The word "inclusion" is confusing, and as a result, there is a lack clarity about what it would look like if fully implemented. We can only make meaning of words based on our own experiences and history attached to the word. I believe the use of the word inclusion and its associated meaning has been evolving, and as a result, the word has described different concepts at different points in time.

Where to from here?

Chapter Six

IMPLEMENTING AN EDUCATION SYSTEM THAT IS INCLUSIVE (KNOWING)

What do we need to know to successfully implement an educational system that is authentically inclusive?

A Common Vision

Embracing systemic changes that enable us to deliver on the agenda of implementing an education system that is inclusive demands that we all agree on a common vision of "the end in mind." Student demographics in our classrooms have changed. Not only are there more and more aspects of diversity identified, but the complexity of these diverse needs has also increased. As a result, in many situations the need is so great that education cannot be expected to manage the delivery of programming exclusively within the system, and must work collaboratively with partners to develop and deliver appropriate programming. This means that the vision for an education system that is inclusive is not a vision for just education, but extends to the community and other systems as well. The vision should describe the natural way in which individuals will work in concert with the system's vision. Everyone should feel that they play an important and necessary role in the work towards achieving the vision. The system leaders are key players in leading the work of systemic change, as a vision for a system that is inclusive is based on values and principles that must be modeled and embedded into the way individuals work within the system.

During the process of developing a vision, consider the following questions:

    a. Be clear about the end in mind. What would you expect it to look like? What is different?
    b. Does the senior leadership and board embrace the vision and lead it?
    c. Does your community know and understand the vision?
    d. Is this vision embedded somehow in your board policy?

Elements to think about:

- Co-create the vision using an engagement strategy: involvement of board, staff, community with respect to vision.
- Develop a three-year implementation plan.
- Establish a leadership advisory committee to guide the development and implementation of a plan for the division.

Communicating High Expectations

Fueling an educational curriculum is the belief that all students are capable of learning. According to Shelly Moore we should always "presume competence."[25] My experience within education has taught me that we have a well-defined pathway through education that we expect typical learners to follow. Based on this pathway, we understand how to measure and report educational success for students. For those students who are not typical

---

[25] Shelley Moore, "Under the Table: The Importance of Presuming Competence," March 11, 2016, presentation, 15:11, *https://www.youtube.com/watch?v=AGptAXTV7m0*.

learners, the pathway is not so clear and as a result the measuring and reporting of their success is not clear either. We need to broaden our perspective about student success and figure out what multiple pathways through education could look like. Imagine a responsive and inclusive curriculum that:

- Anticipates, supports and values diversity.
- Provides multiple ways to access information.
- Creates multiple ways to explore and demonstrate learning.
- Embraces a broad definition of literacy.
- Has clear and robust outcomes that enable teachers to adjust levels of depth, abstraction, and complexity.
- Leverages technology.
- Offers regular and meaningful choices.
- Aligns learning outcomes and competencies across subject areas.
- Uses shared language to support core understandings.
- Provides multiple pathways for student success.

During the process of establishing high expectations consider the following questions:

a. Are all your students connected to the programs of study?
b. Are your teachers comfortable and confident of program delivery for a very diverse population?
c. Where are the gaps? Are there gaps in delivery (*doing*), training and support (*knowing*), or perhaps *believing*?
d. What does success look like?
e. How do you communicate high expectations to the community? To staff?

Capacity Building and Collaborative Practice

Individuals within the system must have clarity regarding their respective roles as they work together. Systemic changes may require new skill sets and new ways of delivering programming. System leaders may ask, "Do staff have the skills, resources and support they need to support the proposed systemic changes?" Education that is inclusive will shift our current system from one that has adapted to meet the needs of atypical learners to one that not only considers them, but also builds a success profile for all students from the beginning of their educational experience. To successfully support a cultural shift and empower staff with the confidence, competence, and comfort required to work differently, leaders and staff must think about what kinds of supports, encouragement, and information are required to build this capacity.

During the process of developing capacity and collaborative practices consider the following questions:

a. What is the level of need within the education community? What needs are arising and how do they manifest? (Frustration, discontent, confusion . . .?)
b. Do staff have the tools, strategies, awareness, etc., to respond to the level of diversity in classrooms?
c. Are individuals prepared to think and work in a different way?
d. Do principals understand that they are guiding this work? Does the executive team see the necessary paradigm shift as the transformational work of implementing an education system that is inclusive? Perhaps leaders must first simply adopt the beliefs that underpin the paradigm shift, and then give permission and support to those who have already demonstrated the necessary beliefs and skills.
e. How will a shared language be introduced to partners?
f. What processes will be put into place to ensure that all partners understand their respective roles, and are all working together to develop a plan in response to an identified need?
g. Has each principal worked with their staff to develop the continuum of support and service available within their site, and is this continuum visually displayed within the school?

h. What is the learning services model and process for identification of strengths and needs?

i. How will the infrastructure within the division be created in order to support the vision and build capacity?

j. How will parents, community members, external support staff, and community agencies be informed or invited to learn the language, beliefs, and practices of the inclusive culture? An example might be through weekly newsletters that capture some of the language as a part of the heading, and then content points that intentionally describe strategies, resources, and activities that demonstrate the inclusive culture.

k. collaborative time must be built into the weekly schedule, e.g., one hour per week, ideally taken from instructional time by shortening each day by twelve minutes.

A Continuum of Supports and Services

When we are clear about high expectations for student success, decisions need to be made about what supports and services are available within the system to support student success. The work of establishing a continuum of supports and services guidelines will provide the guidance necessary that creates expectations about the availability of supports and services for students in the classroom, in their school, or in their community, and across the continuum. We need to consider supports and services also from the perspective of those that will be used universally (all students can use), targeted (a cluster or specific group of students benefit), and finally specialized supports and services (that only a few or individual students require).

According to the document *"Implementing a Continuum of Supports and Services,"* the design of a continuum of supports and services within a division should ensure that they are: learner-centred; strength-based; flexible and responsive; cumulative;

accessible; visible; and integrated.[26] As well, the design of a service delivery model must be seamless, and it must take into consideration school authority deployment and regional deployment of supports and services. In other words, is there a clear understanding of what supports and services are the responsibility of the education system, and which ones are the responsibility of your education partners? The leaders within each school building should engage staff in a collaborative exercise to map out the continuum of supports and services that are available, both internally and externally, to support diverse needs. Once the staff have developed their continuum, a visual display somewhere in the school is necessary as an important frame of reference for this work. Ultimately, the goal should be that families are supported no matter what their entry point is. Success with this process is contingent on educators and professionals having the skills and knowledge to identify and understand the needs of a particular child, so that the response for that child supports their success whether in the classroom, at home, or in the community.

Implementing an education system that is inclusive is transformational. Cultural shifts take time. Future decisions and behaviors must consistently reflect and provide evidence that children and students are all valued to the same degree, and everyone needs to make sure that they are doing this collectively and at all levels of leadership within the system. The decisions and behaviors that reflect valuing all to the same degree are an important and necessary aspect of an education system that is inclusive, where all students and children belong, feel welcomed, and have every opportunity to be successful. A school mantra should be "Everyone feels safe, welcome, and comfortable in our school and community, including visitors, substitute teachers, parents, and community."

---

[26] Alberta Education, *Implementing a Continuum of Supports and Services: A Resource Guide for School and School Authority Leaders*, (Edmonton, Alberta: Alberta Education, 2022), pg. 12

During the design of a continuum of supports and services consider the following:

1. What processes could you use to ensure that a continuum of supports and services is designed and implemented within a division?
2. As a leader, how would you know that a continuum of supports and services is in place and being utilized?

Funding Model

A very good friend who is an internationally known expert in researching and understanding educational funding models once told me that what is valued gets measured, and measured gets funding. Ensure that your education plan has clearly articulated goals reflecting the vision of an educational system that is inclusive. Understand what you will be measuring and reporting on, to ensure that you have the resource infrastructure in place to successfully report on these measures. Decisions need to be made about which supports and services are provided through education and which supports will be deployed through a regional model?

Think about the following:

1. What supports and services will be funded centrally and what supports and services will individual schools be responsible for?
2. How will you determine educational needs within your division to inform deployment of resources equitably?
3. How will you determine what kind of service delivery model needs to be supported within your division?

Accountability and Assurance

Accountability and assurance measures will remind us that we are on course for building an education system that is inclusive. Measures will begin to populate a data collection pool that demonstrates how we are accountable to fulfilling our vision of success for all.

Consider measures that are both qualitative and quantitative in origin. Assurance, for example, are those stories or experiences you can record that instill confidence within your families that you have been successful in delivering on the goals that you have established. Consider the following examples from my personal experience with our son Ben. In his early years at school, I fretted because I did not know if he would be accepted and fit in with the school environment. The educational assistant, at the time, captured moments of Ben's school day as he experienced them throughout the year. At the end of the year Ben's teacher was able to present us with a video of these clips, put to an inspirational tune. As I watched the video my heart was filled and all my worries and anxieties diminished. Ben looked happy, he was engaged in the activities, participating with his fellow students, and a feeling of normalcy was certainly created for us. I felt extremely grateful and was one hundred per cent confident that his program was meeting his needs. His teacher and support staff certainly were meeting the goals and objectives laid out in the program.

However, I worried that Ben's education program would not provide him with the opportunity to learn the necessary skills and tools for his toolbox to allow him to manage independently and successfully within his community. During his elementary years I worked as a vision consultant, supporting teachers who had students identified with visual impairment or blindness in their programs. One of the things I often did as a consultant was bring Ben along on a school visit. The classroom we would be visiting was his age group, and of course one of the students was visually impaired. Ben would offer a presentation to the students, talking about those things that he liked to do and the students were often surprised to find that these things were the things that they also liked to do. As part of the presentation, Ben also identified those things that were necessary for him to participate fully in the classroom. He talked about mobility and accessibility challenges, and offered strategies for the students that they might use to support their classmates.

On our way home, after one such event, Ben reflected that his presentation went very well. So well, in fact, that he expressed the need for Prime Minister Chrétien to know who he was. I agreed and supported his observation that the presentation went extremely well. When we arrived home Ben quickly went to work writing a letter to the prime minister, introducing himself and sharing a little bit of information about where he went to school and some of his strengths and interests. He concluded the letter with an invitation: "So, if you are ever in Edmonton, you need to look me up because you really should meet me." We of course interlined the Braille letter, and then mailed it to Ottawa.

Several weeks later, we received a call from the prime minister's chief of staff. My husband, Roy, immediately held the position that friends were playing a trick on us, pretending that the PM was following up on Ben's letter. As Roy continued to deny the authenticity of the call and the caller continued to insist that the call was legitimate, a truce was finally reached and Roy, in a carefree spirit, jotted down the details of the prime minister's visit to Edmonton and a meeting time and location for us to bring Ben. With amusement and wonder we contemplated what we should do from this point on. Was this really happening?

We had a friend in the RCMP who had responsibility for the security of dignitaries visiting in Edmonton and its surroundings. Perhaps a call to him might provide us with some information as to the prime minister's visit to our city. Roy contacted him and outlined the details of the call, then asked the question: Was the prime minister scheduled to be in Edmonton and if so, was Ben on his itinerary?" Our friend validated the information; yes, the prime minister was scheduled to visit and yes, Ben was on his itinerary. We were off to meet the prime minister!

On the day of the meeting, a couple of things happened. Roy, in his excitement to arrive on time, was stopped by police and received a speeding ticket. When he tried to tell the officer why he was speeding and iterated that he couldn't be delayed—the officer responded in much the same way we had responded to the initial call from the office of the prime minister: Yeah, right! On arrival at the hotel, we were met at the front doors by a couple of security guys who were there to escort us to the meeting. They had an odd smile on their faces and when we inquired if something was wrong, they replied that they had never met anyone who had done a security check on the prime minister prior to a meeting with him. We grew in our level of fame.

The meeting was amazing and a highlight of our life. There was no media or fanfare, just coffee and cake and genuine conversation. Prime Minister Chrétien really wanted to meet our young Ben. On the way out of the meeting, I tried to impress on Ben the magnitude of this event. I told him that he was failing to recognize the significance of this event even happening. I told him that he absolutely needed to write a letter expressing his gratitude for the experience. Ben's response to me was: "Well . . . he was the one wanting to meet me, I think *he* should be thinking about writing *me* a thank-you letter for coming."

Approximately a week after our visit, Ben did receive a thank-you letter, which was in Braille. With very little convincing, Ben wrote his own thank-you letter in reply.

Both qualitative stories were excellent examples, for me, of feedback with respect to Ben's success in education. He was confident, had a strong sense of identity and had skills to support him in living independently within the community. Observing these attributes in my son relaxed my concerns and anxieties about his future, and instilled confidence in me toward the programming he was receiving in his educational program. Qualitative indicators and feedback provide the opportunity for students and families to feel seen and heard, and are vitally important. Consider what an educational environment that is authentically inclusive looks like and feels like. Ensure that you have processes in place to capture the lived experiences and stories of people working and living in these environments.

Consider what stories you will capture and what data you collect to report on the following examples of possible indicators you might have in place:

- All students and families are welcomed, belong, and have authentic opportunities to contribute.

- Principals provide the necessary leadership and support within the school so that staff work together as a unit and the schools operate as a cohesive community.
- Teachers, support staff, service providers, administrators, families, and students have a clear understanding of what success looks like for all.
- There is a focus on competencies.
- There are several educational pathways available to students during their educational journey. Each one of those pathways has clear outcomes, clear reporting mechanisms and equal credentialing as closure on the educational journey.
- Teachers have the capacity and confidence to support diversity by clearly understanding student outcomes more broadly, and have the tools to interpret and adapt programs of study to that end.
- Teachers are monitoring and reporting on student success and therefore student success becomes the focus of conversations.
- Families are engaged in the educational process and are involved in conversations about their child's success.
- Guidelines that outline the supports and services expected to become a natural part of the learning environment are in place, and a funding formula defines the expected availability of these supports and services.
- Service providers have become an integral part of the school team. Teachers have the capacity to identify supports and services that are necessary for student success, and have a clear understanding of the planning process to access and embed these supports and services into the delivery of educational programs.
- Coaching and mentoring have become an important aspect of working within the educational environment.
- Technology is embedded in planning, infused in educational processes, and embraced as part of the inclusive educational philosophy.

- The school day, term, or year may look different. Expect that time is built into the system in order to provide the necessary opportunities for collaboration, coaching, and teaming.
- The school environment may look different. Expect showcasing of a range of supports, resources, and services so that teachers can essentially shop to find just the right fit for one of their students.
- Spaces to support teaming, collaboration, and experiential learning opportunities are evident, and accessibility for all students has become an issue of the past.

In my efforts to effect change within educational environments I was influenced by the publication *IHI Psychology of Change Framework: to Advance and Sustain Improvement*. This white paper was written for all leaders interested in understanding the underlying psychology of change and leveraging its power to impact quality improvement efforts. This paper outlines and unpacks five interconnected domains of practice: unleash intrinsic motivation; co-design people-driven change; co-produce in authentic relationships; and distribute power and adapt in action. I loved this paper because the work is based on psychology, which is the understanding of how people think and feel and what motivates them. A powerful statement from this paper that resonated with me, when I pondered about the barriers preventing us from successfully implementing education environments that are inclusive, was "Resistance is the judgement made by the brain that the proposal for change threatens what people are currently doing." [27] This is a wonderful paper to support an understanding of human behavior as implementation planning occurs.

---

[27] K. Hilton and A. Anderson, *IHI Psychology of Change Framework to Advance and Sustain Improvement*, (Boston, Massachusetts: Institute for Healthcare Improvement; 2018), pg. 5. *https://www.ihi.org/resources/Pages/IHIWhitePapers/IHI-Psychology-of-Change-Framework.aspx*

Chapter Seven

BUILDING TEAMS AND COMMUNITY (DOING)

We work in a complex human system; however, embracing a collaborative approach to problem solving helps us move further along with creating educational environments that are inclusive. According to *Participating Effectively as a Collaborative Partner: A United Way Toronto Toolkit,* the definition of collaboration is:

> **Two or more different partners (e.g., individuals, organizations, networks) coming together from various sectors, groups and/or neighbourhoods to work together toward common goals. Collaborations are about people and organizations building, nurturing, and maintaining mutually beneficial relationships in order to achieve shared goals that will benefit all partners. [28]**

The success of a collaborative process is dependent on healthy relationships. I was fortunate enough to have a wellness coordinator, Felicia Och, as a member of my team within our school division. This position was important because she took the

---

[28] Heather Graham and Linda Mollenhauer, *Participating Effectively as a Collaborative Partner: A United Way Toronto Toolkit* (Toronto, Ontario: United Way Toronto, 2011), pg. 7.

opportunity to foster relationships and partnerships within the division and within the community at large. She understood the importance and value in relationships and embraced the concept of "It takes a village to raise a child." Data and research support the notion that our classrooms today are becoming more and more complex, not only in numbers of diverse needs, but in the complexity of those needs.

When I was leading the work of "Setting the Direction," Albertans expressed their concern about the need for education to establish partnerships to design programs within education that were responsive to need. I heard over and over that education should no longer believe that it should go this journey alone. Felicia provided the necessary leadership to chart our path through the development of community partnerships and designed processes that facilitated collaborative efforts of the work.

In the fall of 2016, my colleague Leah Andrews and I wrote an article for *The CASS Connection*, the magazine of the College of Alberta School Superintendents, called "Walking Together Towards Inclusive Education."[29] In the article we talked about our work of moving our division forward in the areas of wellness, inclusion, and quality learning, and how we were doing this work together. We incorporated the following quote from our wellness coordinator, who always reminded us to embrace stillness:

> *Let's imagine time could be stopped just long enough so that we could all hold onto and bottle up the sense of well-being we experience when we're doing exactly what we love. If we had the ability to maintain a sense of well-being in everything we do and extend that feeling to all those with whom we come in contact, we would certainly*

---

[29] Dianne McConnell and Leah Andrews, "Walking Together Towards Inclusive Education," *The CASS Connection*, 12, no. 2., (Fall 2016): 17- *19*

ensure all students were experiencing success and well-being.[30]

Following are some examples of how we did this work.

Implementing Comprehensive School Health

Our journey towards integrating wellness into our school communities began with Felicia pulling together one member from each of our schools. She supported them in the implementation of Alberta Education's Comprehensive School Health Curriculum. This initiative was supported through grant money from the University of Alberta and an expectation of this work was the development of a school action plan identifying how the school was going to integrate the four pillars—social and physical environment, teaching and learning, healthy school policy, and partnerships and services—of the comprehensive school health curriculum into the culture of their respective schools. Many wonderful initiatives resulted from this work, including:

- Schools offering support through collaborative, responsive teams, with identified staff members (teachers) who served as Inclusive Education Leads, supporting students, parents, and co-workers.
- School staff members connecting students and families to the next step in support and functioning as bridge builders. We called them "health champions."
- CHANGE Health Clinic: A part-time medical team providing service in the school to support students and their families and connect them with the health care system. The work focused on nutrition, fitness, mental health, strong relationships, and community connections.

---

[30] Dianne McConnell and Leah Andrews, "Walking Together Towards Inclusive Education," *The CASS Connection*, 12, no. 2., (Fall 2016): pg. *19*.

- Community Connectors: In partnership with our local primary care network, we accessed grant money to create and fund Community Connector positions that supported local youth, ages 11–25, and their families in accessing and navigating community mental health supports and services. Staff in this position collaborated with community members, social service agencies, and health care.
- We designed community advisory groups with specialized health partners to work with education collaboratively, in order to find innovative ways to support students and families with identified mental health needs.
- Numerous organizations and businesses throughout the Edmonton Tri-Municipal Region joined us to facilitate the creation of environments where students feel supported emotionally and physically. Youth wellness creates ripples that affect everyone in the community. It increases positive connections, happiness, safety, health, and well-being for all.

Felicia accessed several grants to support physical literacy, nutrition, and mental health for our students.

Change Health

I had the good fortune of meeting an innovative and creative family doctor, Dr. Doug Klein, who was in the process of moving a CHANGE Health agenda forward. His research focused on metabolic rehabilitation—in layman's language, preventive health care—hence the name, which reflects changing health care from a reactive to a proactive paradigm.

Countless studies show that growing numbers of Canadians lead increasingly unhealthy lives. Whether this is because of their busy lifestyles that require more time sitting in cars and in front of screens, or they lack knowledge about how to purchase and prepare healthy foods, the situation is complex and requires the investment of diverse systems leaders. In the past, children and adults would spend several hours each week outdoors. This is no longer the case. In his book, *Last Child in the Woods, Saving Our Children from Nature-Deficit Disorder*, child advocacy expert, Richard Louv directly links the lack of nature in the lives of today's wired generation to some concerning childhood trends. For today's generation, nature is found on YouTube or Wikipedia, rather than through actual experience. This disconnection with nature may be contributing to increasing rates of mental health problems, chronic disease, and the obesity crisis that Canada currently faces.

In Canada, like every other developed economy, we are responding to this crisis by **spending increasing amounts of money on health care, although what we are really buying is disease care**. Something change—and CHANGE Health is working to create a new collaborative model of health service delivery that supports preventive, personalized, and community-relevant care to Albertans.

CHANGE Health is a customized approach to health supported by an inter-professional team focusing on families' specific needs. The principles are:

- customized nutrition and graded exercise intervention (tailored to family preferences and abilities);
- supervision and implementation of the program in a collaborative fashion between the family and the CHANGE Health Team (family doctor, dietitian, kinesiologist, teacher, social worker, and psychologist);
- focus on mental health, family attachment, and social connection.

The program links with community resources including schools, community centres, local family programs, libraries, and local businesses such as grocery stores and recreation facilities. There is also an embedded evaluation component to capture the CHANGE Health Community Program's real-world impact, and to inform future developments in order to optimize the program's value to families, communities, and the Alberta health ecosystem.

The vision of CHANGE Health is to be widely-recognized as Canada's leading health protection and improvement program for both adults, children, and families through collaboration with government, educators, health care, businesses, and community leaders.

I first became involved with Dr. Klein when he approached our school division and expressed an interest in working within one of our schools. We were excited by the opportunities that this would create for our students, of having a family physician onsite one day per week. An initial goal was to provide the opportunity for every student to have a connection with a primary care doctor. As the work evolved, Dr. Klein introduced many activities and opportunities for the students and staff. For example, on his scheduled days in the school, he showed up early and invited students to join him in an early-morning basketball game. Teachers connected with him and asked him to join them in the delivery of relevant aspects of the high school Career and Life Management (CALM) curriculum. As our partnership grew and evolved, he connected with several other schools and brought families together in the school after hours for a family camp experience. These family camps focused on connecting community members with programs that built life skills to support lifelong healthy nutrition, active lifestyles, mental well-being, and positive social connections, moving them from a mindset of disease care to true health care.

CHANGE Health was established to support Alberta families to build life skills in four core areas:

a. Nutrition and meal preparation
b. Physical activity and lifelong fitness
c. Mental health and well-being
d. Strong partner and family relationships, and community connections

By co-designing solutions with authentic partnerships, CHANGE Health supports Alberta families in learning, or for most of us, re-learning healthy living through lifelong healthy nutrition, active lifestyles, and positive social connections. He embraced collaboration and partnership in this work and believed that he and his team needed to have a presence within schools to effect and influence change.

Together we proposed the creation of a **CHANGE Centre**, a provincial innovation hub located in our community, focusing on a new model of health and education delivery, training, evaluation, and research. We envisioned that the CHANGE Centre would be a joint-use space between the health and education sectors as well as the community, facilitating the expansion of the existing work of CHANGE Health.

At this time the CHANGE Health model had received $1 million to fund programs for families in the community, some of which, we proposed, could be conducted out of the CHANGE Centre. We had a commitment of additional funding over the next four years and funding for CHANGE Health programming in the workplace. What was lacking for us was a joint-use facility to support a field laboratory, where diverse partners from across systems could learn together how to address complex social issues; a space for multi-disciplinary collaboration; and strategies for addressing complex challenges that are co-designed by those with lived experience (i.e., community members, patients, teachers, students, and staff).

Building on existing partnerships between health care and education, the CHANGE Centre was expected to support the community by:

- Creating multi-partner relationships that authentically bridge perspectives and systems;
- Empowering communities to design, facilitate and evaluate solutions;
- Delivering these co-designed solutions with community partners; and
- Demonstrating how family medicine can work collaboratively with communities to create and protect health.

Zai Hassan, in *The Social Labs Fieldbook* says:

Complex social challenges are emergent [constantly changing and forming in new ways] because their properties arise from the interaction of many parts. Imagine the difference between throwing a rock and throwing a live bird. The rock will follow a path that is predictable, that is, it can be predicted with a high degree of accuracy in advance. The path of the bird, on the other hand, is emergent, which means that path cannot be predicted in advance. [31]

Dr. Klein believes that healthcare professionals have a place in our educational system and is working in several of our schools. By working closely with him, I have learned the following important principles:

1. Healthcare providers need to be where children and youth are.
2. **Healthcare providers need to understand the educational culture.**
3. Healthcare providers can assist in building capacity within the educational workforce and youth by influencing quality life choices specific to nutrition, physical literacy, and mental health.
4. Healthcare providers can assist in connection and navigation through health care and social services systems
5. The presence of healthcare professionals in educational settings changes the relationship with individuals' perspectives or perceptions specific to accessing health care services.
6. Healthcare providers influence a focus on proactive/early intervention strategies and choices.

---

[31] Zaid Hassan, The Social Labs Fieldbook, (San Francisco: Berrett-Koehler Publishers, 2014), pg. 9. *https://social-labs.org/fieldbook/*

I was excited, passionate, and hopeful about this work. It was a privilege to be a part of it.

Change Summit and Achieving Community Together (ACT)

In 2015, Felicia and some important partners started talking about the strengths of our community. They began to look at how community and health are linked, and found there was a growing appetite to work differently, maybe even live differently.

They invited people from every walk of life in the community, to start having community conversations. Residents, government employees, physicians, educators, youth, service providers, municipal employees, spiritual leaders, volunteers, and private business owners from the City of Spruce Grove, Parkland County, Paul First Nation, and the Town of Stony Plain al participated. The first formal conversation was called the "Change Summit," and was facilitated by Paul Born, President of the Tamarack Institute for Community Engagement. It was held in November, 2016.

Participants were assured that they were heard and slowly they learned how community conversations can deepen their relationships and transform the community they love. Following is a summary of what they heard at the Change Summit.

Participants collectively committed to listening to and learning from their community while at the same time respecting the diversity of the people who make up their community. Their overarching goal was to agree on a collective vision of creating a happy, healthy, vibrant community where they all would work and play. They embraced the concept of designing and experimenting with social innovation, and were committed to developing a deep sense of belonging for each community member. They believed that by committing to working and engaging in a different way, they could deepen their connection and they could move toward a new understanding of community.

Throughout the Change Summit the participants were guided by the following definitions, and adopted the desired state as their vision for the end in mind.

Definitions of Community:

CURRENT STATE: a group of people living in the same place or having a particular characteristic in common; i.e., community as defined by our geographical and political boundaries.
DESIRED STATE: a feeling of fellowship with others, as a result of sharing common attitudes, interests, and goals; i.e., community is defined by a sense of feeling.

Regardless of where they came from, they committed to the following:

- Connecting—to create platforms and feedback loops for their community to share and learn.
- Being inclusive—to make sure all voices within the community are heard.
- Building the capacity of coalition partners—to focus on building our partners' capacity, not our own sources of funding/partnerships to support our work.
- Keeping a small footprint—to leverage existing assets and remove the duplication of programming and activities.
- Bringing in additional human and economic resources and maximizing shared resources and to find new sources of funding/partnerships to support our work.
- Make the movement visible and accessible to the public—to be the face and resource for their community issues through transparency and inclusiveness in their work.
- Authentically collaborate—to build meaningful, sustainable, and productive relationships that deepened their community.

Paul Born, cofounder and President of Tamarack- An Institute for Community Engagement, says:

"The real hope offered by community conversations is not dramatic change. Rather, it is establishing a new set of relationships that, over time, become the norm. In any community effort, the people involved learn to work together to realize a desired vision. By collaborating, people establish a new set of authentic relationships that become the norm. They learn because they are motivated by the vision. And as they learn, they change. We begin to see the transcendent impact of collaboration as we see its effects on organizations, the lives of individuals, and the community."[32]

Interestingly, some of the strategies the community agreed to implement included:

- Creating spaces for conversations to happen with our neighbours in our neighbourhoods, in our facilities, and in our businesses. Plan two additional summits: one by our younger residents (under age 30) and the other by Paul First Nations so that we can learn more.
- Gathering regularly to listen to our neighbours throughout 2017, in order to understand how we might do little things every day that result in large-scale social change.
- Collaborate to create the **Community Compass**, a web-based resource linking citizens with the local resources already available.

Through the experience of the summit the community partners also articulated the desired end-states in areas of health, transportation, social issues, and learning.

The Desired State of Health:

- Improving social connectivity that reflects our sense of belonging and is recognized as one of the least addressed

---

[32] Paul Born, Community Conversations pg. 79

yet most important aspects of health, especially mental health.

- The first step that someone takes towards getting help will be the right one, regardless of where they reach out for help (school, doctor's office, library, grocery store, government office); this community will respond with compassion towards an expression of need.
- The physical layout of our community must support access for all to the essential amenities of daily living, and must include public spaces where social connectivity is possible and occurs naturally.
- The way we design our communities will result in measurable improved health and social connectivity.
- Make health care an integrated, accessible part of the community and, as much as possible, address the determinants of health without creating separate silos of institutionalized (and isolating) care.

The Desired State of Transportation:

- Transportation options that connect this entire region.
- Infrastructure planning that is coordinated to incorporate not only motorized (passive), but also non-motorized (active) transportation (e.g., walking, cycling, skateboarding).
- Public transportation that increases access to essential services and the amenities of daily living for all (e.g., young adults, seniors unable to drive, lower income, and individuals with disabilities).
- The transportation solutions will support balanced thinking between our present needs as well as the ecological and long-term impact of our design.

The Desired State of Learning:

- Holistic learning that acknowledges the mind, body, emotions, and spirit of the person.

- Learning happening everywhere in this community.
- Learning that takes place through intentional storytelling.
- Learning that happens by doing, playing, and exploring new spaces in this community.
- All ages will show that they are learning.
- Learning will be measured by the amount of generosity expressed by the learner.

The desired state of learning also includes the opportunity for all citizens to be involved with pursuits they like, that they have a desire to learn and achieve more and could have a passion for, and includes structures or support for these interests to be pursued at high levels of success for the individual.

The Desired State of Social Issues:

- We will move from feelings of fear to safety by building relationships.
- We will be intentional about including those who are unfamiliar to us.
- We will value diversity and respect individual beliefs.
- We will regularly see expressions of gratitude for our community, the people who make it great, and the businesses and organizations who demonstrate that they value ALL people.

The overall belief from the community members was that community shapes their identity and directly impacts the health and well-being of all its citizens.

How Are We Measuring Our Impact?

If they measure what they treasure . . . then generosity is what they are looking for; a sense of humility within our community. Will the average person experience more generosity in this community? Will we model more generosity in how we live, work, and use our time?

Real change takes time. Their time moving forward will be spent intentionally deepening the relationships and connections within their communities, and their primary strategy will be to engage through listening.

Achieving Community Together became formalized in the months following the summit and exists today as a small group continuing to champion the work of collaboration, partnership, and relationships to create a vibrant, healthy community.

Community Connectors

At a personal level, our family journey was extremely rare and very complex, and you can imagine there is a tremendous amount of information between the lines. The bottom line, however, and an important aspect not to lose sight of, is that our journey was ongoing (over the span of thirty-plus years), multifaceted, and with multisystem involvement.

The health challenges our boys faced were difficult for our family to manage emotionally and practically. Our future was unknown and scary, and it took an extreme amount of energy each day to establish normalized life experiences. Erik and Ben suffered from a very unforgiving genetic disorder. They faced significant challenges throughout their lives, and as a family, we moved from one specialist to another, from one hospital ward to another, and from one system to another. Throughout their journey, our family was challenged by gaps in the systems, walls between mandates, and always, always, protocols, processes, and procedures.

Ben was admitted to the University of Alberta Hospital in Edmonton at the end of June; at the same time, Erik was admitted to the Grey Nuns Hospital, also in Edmonton. During this time both had admissions to the Intensive Care Units. Roy and I spent each day travelling from one hospital to the other, about 45 minutes one way, in order to support both boys. During this time, we had many, many conversations with the hospital staff about how we could get Erik transferred from the Grey Nuns to the University Hospital. It did not make any sense to us why we could not get any support for this request. The boys had the same complex diagnosis, and our family was trying to negotiate and manage two completely different healthcare teams.

After almost two months of this routine, I contacted the executive staff of Alberta Health Services to plead my case and ask for support to get Erik moved. Our bid was successful and Erik was moved almost immediately, but another wonderful thing happened. The executive that we talked to demonstrated a genuine interest in our circumstances and as a result, we were introduced to a "systems navigator."

Introducing the systems navigator into our family was a powerful and remarkable turning point for us, and at the time of our first meeting, I had no idea of the magnitude of the impact we had experienced. **She became our constant, the known entity in the day-to-day management of our journey. She grew to really know each member of our family. She listened and grasped what we were worrying about or perceiving as a challenge at any given moment. She introduced herself to us as a "hope carrier" because she said that when she first met us, she sensed that we were losing hope and it was her responsibility to hold hope for us. We felt seen, heard, cared for, and really connected to those we needed to be connected to.**

Aside from spending time getting to know us and becoming aware of our needs, she was also connected to the systems we depended on. She had permission and an invitation to work across systems and intentionally connect them. After each of her visits with us, she followed up with an email to all the professionals involved with our family. They grew to know us in a different way. For example, one of Ben's doctors reported, "I didn't know the McConnell's had another son with the same diagnosis." Our beloved navigator removed barriers and facilitated opportunities— she was our Hope Carrier. The beautiful thing for me is that I noticed a shift in my own well-being. I no longer had a focus on an external locus of control and I started to view myself as part of the solution. My capacity grew, and I saw myself doing things I never imagined I would be able to do. A great example is that I was able to manage Ben's tracheostomy at home. A tracheostomy is a surgically created hole (stoma) in the windpipe that provides an alternative airway for breathing. It requires close monitoring and occasional suctioning to clear the airway.

The navigator allowed us to support Ben in our home, unlike our experience trying to support Erik. We believed at the time that we did not have the capacity to support him at home and as a result, he lived in an assisted-living facility. Our locus of control had shifted from external (the solution is outside of us, someone else is going to fix this) to internal (we saw ourselves as part of the solution). Believing that you are part of the solution builds your capacity in responding.

As a result of our experience, I strongly believe that embedding system navigators or community connectors into our education and health care systems would enhance the quality of life for families as well as the rewards of effective and efficient service delivery and care.

Working with the systems navigator empowered me to become part of the solution for complex issues and problems. As a result, my thinking shifted, which enabled me to see opportunities that opened doors to possibilities. My decisions and behaviors became more proactive in nature and I was no longer sitting around waiting to react to the next acute event.

The role of the Community Connector or navigator is necessary to support the transformational changes we want to see happening. They can be the hope carriers providing navigational support to schools, staff, families, and students, ensuring the right supports and services are available when needed and for the duration and intensity needed. They work fluidly across systems, creating effective and efficient deployment of resources and they support individuals in seeing themselves as a vital and necessary piece of the solution.

Collaborations Should Be Enabled

Perhaps, when we really know our students, know ourselves, and invite partners to work collaboratively with us, we may be better able to respond to the diverse needs in all our classrooms. Alberta Education published *Working Together: Collaborative Practices and Partnership Toolkit*[33] in 2013 to assist partners in developing effective and authentic collaborative processes. This document identifies collaboration as an overlapping continuum that involves networking (exchanging information), cooperating (on some tasks with shared goals), and integrating (programs or organizations). I found this document especially helpful as a guide when we were faced with complex issues or problems to be solved.

The benefits of being involved with successful collaborative efforts meant that we no longer tackled adverse situations alone, and efficiencies and effective use of resources occurred. The unintended benefits or consequences were that trusting relationships were formed, individuals reported a better sense of well-being, and feelings of belonging were generated.

Questions to consider:

1. What processes could you employ to inspire community partners to partner with education systems?
2. Have you identified a process for identifying and accessing grant money to support collaborative partnerships?
3. What processes could you have in place to ensure that collaborative partnerships are successful?

---

[33] Alberta Education, *Working together: collaborative practices and partnership toolkit: supporting Alberta Students*, (Edmonton: Alberta Education, 2013), *https://open.alberta.ca/dataset/6927719-english*.

Chapter Eight

EVIDENCE

An education system that is inclusive is built on principles and values rather than compliance and processes. The information we gather is determined by those goals and objectives we measure. Transformation is messy and as we design a system that is inclusive, we should do so by identifying both quantitative and qualitative information that provides us with the accountability and assurance that we are moving towards our end in mind. The model should be driven by a mindset of continuous improvement which provides us with the confidence to make the adjustments and changes that keep us on the right path.

So, what kinds of information should we measure and gather?

Qualitative Indicators as Demonstrated Through Story.

I shared earlier that when our son Ben was in elementary school and I was worrying about whether he fit in, his teacher and educational assistant made and shared a video with me that completely put me at ease. This action on their part provided the assurance that his educational program was on track and he was experiencing success.

There were many more examples from our experience that became important indicators of a system that was truly fostering belonging and a strong sense of identity for him. Later in Ben's elementary journey, I received a panicked call from the school alerting me to the fact that Ben had just shown up at the beginning of the year school patrol meeting, reporting to the teachers that he wanted to join the school patrol team. The staff were alarmed and were not sure what to do, and that resulted in them calling me. They could not envision how to support Ben in his desire to be one of the team that enters traffic and stops it to make the street crossing safe for students. They shared with me their thoughts, which were along the lines of "After all, he is blind, and what would all the other parents think?"

When I received the call, I asked them if they had asked Ben why he wanted to be in the school patrol; they responded that they had not, and assured me they would. When they did ask him why he wanted to be a member of the team, he replied that he knew the patrols had a party at the end of the year and he did not want to miss the party. The staff relaxed and thought of a way for him to belong. They assigned him the role of manager, and his job was to call the patrols assigned for duty each day to remind them of the schedule. He loved the power of his job and truly experienced the feeling of belonging.

When he was in high school, he was determined to join his peers at the Rotary meetings that recruited students for possible youth exchange opportunities. He was determined to become an exchange student, and did not miss any of the proposed meetings. What we did not know was that at the time, Rotary had never engaged in the process of exchanging a student with an identified disability. We learned later that when Ben continued to demonstrate that he was determined to participate, they called a special meeting to discuss how they were going to manage this situation. They were deciding whether they would venture forward and chart a new path for Rotary, or tell me he was not a viable candidate and ask him to stop coming to the meetings. Fortunately, they decided to support him and began to design new processes and protocols to support a successful exchange. A very special thank you to those amazing Rotarians, because Ben did go on that exchange—to Recife, Brazil, no less!

Students that have the educational experience of being seen and heard feel that they belong. They see the opportunities in the contribution of their strengths and talents, develop confidence, and a strong sense of self or positive identity. Ben believed he could do the things he wanted to do and had the confidence to dream the dream. He wanted to travel and live independently as a young person, and so he did. He applied for and was accepted to university at Carleton University in Ottawa. When it came time for him to leave for the university, his dad accompanied him to support his orientation on campus. Very shortly after his dad left to return home, I received a call from Ben and he was in a panic. On the other end of the phone, from the other side of the country, I heard, "Mom, Mom, did you know I have a disability?" Curious, I asked what made him ask that question and he replied, "I just discovered I can't figure out how to find the cafeteria." Reflecting on that conversation, I am convinced Ben had a strong sense of self and saw himself as capable as anyone else—once he figured out the cafeteria challenge.

During his tenure at Carleton, he applied for a third-year exchange to Stirling, Scotland, and was accepted. He managed the year in Scotland and absolutely loved being there. When he graduated, he applied to law school in Victoria, British Columbia, and was accepted. Three years later he graduated with his law degree and applied for articles in Edmonton. After a year of articles, he was called to the bar and we enjoyed a wonderful celebration with him.

Al Etmanski shares the story *"What Ted and Josh Kuntz Taught Me,"* in his book, *The Power of Disability*[34]. The story references Ted Kuntz's reflection of his son's experience in school. Ted is the father of Josh Kuntz, a boy with a serious seizure disorder as a result of a reaction to a vaccine. Josh's intellectual development and language were also affected. As part of Ted's reflection, he recounts an incident that occurred

---

[34] Al Etmanski, *The Power of Disability: 10 lessons for surviving, thriving, and changing the world,* (Oakland, CA: Berrett-Koehler Publishers, Inc., 2020), 73.

when Josh was entering Grade 7. Two Grade 7 teachers met to divide the seventy Grade 7 students into two classes; they decided they would do this by flipping a coin. Before they began the process, one of the teachers picked Josh and the other was curious why he would pick a student with a severe disability as his first choice. The teacher replied with the following comment, "I think having Josh in my class will make it a kinder and gentler place for everyone. I have been around the school for several years and I noticed how the other children respond to Josh. I noticed they were eager to greet him when they passed him in the hallways. I noticed children modifying games to include him, and comforting him after a seizure." Ted and Josh's teacher both expressed the benefits of embracing the value and contribution of every student. Josh's teacher expressed that he felt having Josh in his class helped his students become better citizens.

There are many ways a system can gather stories that emulate the vision of a welcoming, caring and belonging experience. Parents provide feedback and tell their stories in community, or give feedback to the school staff through expressions of gratitude. I once had a custodial staff member recall a story to me about a student that she deemed a "miracle case." This staff member worked in a school where she witnessed this student having extreme difficulty, which led to engaging in self harm and aggressive behaviors. As the school staff grew to understand the student's needs and had appropriate responses in place to support her, she improved significantly. Both the staff member and the student moved schools and it was sometime later that they met again. This caretaking staff member was shocked at the improvement she saw in the little girl, and rushed to share this experience with me.

Schools can intentionally design mechanisms and processes to gather qualitative feedback. Parent and student surveys asking for feedback about their experiences and feelings are good examples. So are engagement opportunities to hear from students, parents, and community members, asking them for feedback on your vision and strategies for implementation. A good question to ask is, "How are we doing?" A promising practice embedded in your engagement events is to follow up with a mechanism to provide feedback and validate "what we heard." Consider and then identify what your feedback loops will be, so that they provide you with the information you need to make necessary course corrections.

In 2016, Richard Villa and Jacqueline Thousand published, *"The Inclusive Education Checklist: A self -assessment of best practices*[35]*."* Using a resource of this nature not only guides you in making the pedagogical shifts necessary to implement an education system that is inclusive; it also provides you with evidence of researched best practices in place that support you in reporting how your division is designed to support all students.

Quantitative Data

Think about what data you will gather at the school level, within the division, and within the community. The information you collect and report on should focus on continuous improvement and provide the assurance that you are delivering on the goals specific to implementing an educational system that is inclusive.

As you make decisions about what you are going to measure, collect, and report, think about the kinds of assessment tools that are being used across the division and within classrooms. As student achievement is reported, does your system have a mechanism in place that ensures that reporting on all students is connected to the programs of study?

Research has shown that there has been a rise in mental health concerns within our student and staff population in the aftermath of the COVID lockdown. Also, our student demographics have been changing over the years, and we know that diversity has increased not only in numbers but also complexity. Evidence of the

---

[35] Richard Villa and Jacqueline Thousand, *The Inclusive Education Checklist: A self-assessment of best practices*, (Katonah, NY: Dude Publishing, 2016).

impact of adversity can be collected through mechanisms such as reporting regularly on student and staff attendance, the number of suspensions and expulsions, human rights complaints, and participation numbers in surveys and engagement opportunities. As you shift from transactional to transformational practices you will likely see an improvement in these areas, which provides evidence that what you are doing is making a difference.

Questions to consider:

1. What evidence could you gather at the classroom, school, division, and community level to provide the assurance to a board or community that you are meeting the outlined goals in the education plan?
2. What processes could you have in place to report the findings of your data collected?

Inclusion: A Call to Action

A call to action is information encouraging and influencing an audience to take some specific action. The purpose is to convince the audience to choose a particular option, either by creating a sense of urgency or providing information illustrating why and how the recommended choice is best. It encourages one to do something, by providing relevant information and examples, and incorporates specific action words that clarify how to become involved in this task. Hence: *being, knowing,* and *doing.*

I believe we are listening to this call to action and beginning the journey to design educational environments and programs that are inclusive. In the fall of 2022, Alberta Education released the document *Implementing a Continuum of Supports and Services.* The document is intended to do the following:

- Guide school leaders to support the implementation of the outlined principles of inclusion, the Education Act, and Professional Standards;
- Develop a shared understanding of the principles and conditions in a continuum of supports and services;

- Highlight the knowledge, skills, and understanding schools and school authority leaders demonstrate to create the conditions for success;
- Outline roles and responsibilities, all through the lenses of *being, knowing* and *doing* inclusion.[36]

The document is written as a guide for implementing educational environments that are inclusive through the lenses of *being, knowing,* and *doing.* An education system that is inclusive needs to be built from a principle-and-values approach, and according to Alberta Education's policy on inclusion, ". . .demonstrates universal acceptance and belonging, and embraces diversity and differences to promote equitable opportunities for each learner."[37]

On page 9 of the document, the second paragraph says, "How we show up each day matters. *Being* underlies how our personal character, identity and beliefs are authentically immersed in our day-to-day interactions. It is the being that connects teachers with their learners, and leaders with their school community [. . .] Educational leaders who demonstrate being provide the foundational need for belonging, a key principle of inclusive education in Alberta."[38]

I believe our end in mind must be focused on the belief that everyone deserves to have a life in which they thrive. According to Al Etmanski:

A thriving life must be accompanied by a nurturing environment that includes family and friends who care about you and a society that cares about you too—cares enough to allocate resources,

---

[36] *https://open.alberta.ca/publications/implementing-continuum-supports-services-resource-guide-school.* Pg 7

[37] https://www.alberta.ca/guide-to-education.aspx

[38] *https://open.alberta.ca/publications/implementing-continuum-supports-services-resource-guide-school.* Pg 9

provide opportunities, and expand justice so that you can live life to the fullest.[39]

He goes on to say, "There is only one world and if we are going to preserve it, we have to make it a place where people are enlarged, not threatened by difference."[40] Shelley Moore's book, *One Without the Other,* promotes the same concept.

There are many wonderful examples of individuals who have answered the inclusion call to action. Kirsteen Main is a Canadian poet who composes using an alphabet board, a device that enables her to gesture in the direction of the letter she has chosen; she wrote, "not being able to speak is not the same as not having anything to say."[41] It is important for us to pay attention to the voice of individuals that have faced adversity with dignity and grace. My son wrote the following song shortly before he passed away.

> Could this be Grace?
> Could this be Grace?
> I've been searching all over the place
> From people's stories, to their many actions
> I can see it in their face.
>
> Could this be Grace?
> It's so interlaced
> With pain and suffering, or fear of trying
> It's hard to see through their tears and their crying
>
> But through all the trials
> And unexpected self-doubts
> Oh, Grace can be found, if you look around

---

[39] Etmanski, *The Power of Disability,* pg. 157.
[40] Etmanski, *The Power of Disability,* pg. 158.
[41] Etmanski, The Power of Disability pg. 153

We can find it in ourselves

Could this be Grace?
That's changing my heart and my soul
Oh, could this be Grace, giving me courage
And reminding me I am whole

Could this be the chance?
I need to see
When Grace leads me to open my heart and it inspires my soul

Could this be Grace?
I've been searching all over the place
From people's stories, to their many actions
I can see it in their face

Could this be Grace?
That's changing my heart and my soul
Oh, could this be Grace, giving me courage
And reminding me I am whole[42]

As I worked on my doctoral research, I was surrounded by individuals who supported me, believed in me, and truly created a sense of belonging for me. When I completed my research and finished my dissertation, I inserted the following tribute to them.

Imagine a world where everyone has the experience of feeling that they belong. Do the work of examining the beliefs that fuel your decisions and actions (know thyself) and create a compassionate space between you and others (know the other). This call to action will result in educational environments that are inclusive as a natural way in which we work. According to Deborah Dagit, who lived for months at a time in hospitals and eventually became a

---

[42] Erik McConnell, 2016

disability advocate, "Regardless of our age and station in life, all of us can be leaders if we acknowledge and share the knowledge we uniquely have, to help other's paths become easier."[43]

When you decide that an inclusive education system is the place where you want to live and work, find the things you need to know to be successful and then engage or do the actions, behaviors, and decisions that support that vision.

Do not just dream the dream—make it a reality.

---

[43] Etmanski, The Power of Disability pg. 82-83

Bibliography

Books

Al Etmanski, *The Power of Disability: 10 lessons for surviving, thriving, and changing the world.* (Berrett-Koehler Publishers, Inc., 2020).

Baldwin Ross Hergenhahn, *An Introduction to Theories of Learning*, (NJ: Prentice Hall, 1988)

David Irvine, *The Other Everest: Navigating the Pathway to Authentic Leadership.* (Calgary, AB: Gondolier, an imprint of Bayeux Arts Digital – Traditional Publishing, 2018).

Dianne McConnell, *School Experiences of Successful Adults with Blindness*, (Doctoral Dissertation. Edmonton: University of Alberta, 1997).

Dianne McConnell, *Could this be Grace? A question that helps us gain strength and see opportunity in the face of adversity.* (Stouffville, ON: Black Card Books, 2022).

Gordon Neufeld and Gabor Maté, *Hold on to Your Kids: Why Parents Need to Matter More Than Peers,* (Toronto: Vintage Canada, 2004).

Maren Hasse, *Fierce Integrity,* (The Difference Press, Washington, DC. 2013).

Miguel Ruiz, *The Four Agreements.* (San Rafael, CA: Amber-Allen Publishing, Inc., 1997).

Miguel Ruiz, Jose Ruiz, Janet Mills, *The Fifth Agreement.* (San Rafael, CA: Amber-Allan Publishing, Inc., 2010).

Mike Dooley, *Infinite Possibilities: The Art of Changing your Dreams*. New York, (NY: Atria Paperback/Beyond Words – a division of Simon and Schuster, Inc. 2019).

Mike Dooley, *Infinite Possibilities; The Art of Changing your Life Workbook,* (TUT Enterprises Inc. 2014).

Paul, Born, *Community Conversations: Mobilizing the Ideas, Skills, and Passion of Community Organizations,* (BPS Books, Toronto, and New York, 2012).

Richard Villa, Jacqueline Thousand, *The Inclusive Education Checklist: A self-assessment of best practices*. (Katonah, NY: Dude Publishing, 2016).

Richard, Louv, *Last Child in the Woods: Saving Our Children from Nature-Deficit Disorder*, (Algonquin Books, Chapel Hill, North Carolina, 2008).

Ronald Hulnick, Mary Hulnick, *Loyalty to Your Soul: The Heart of Spiritual Psychology, (Hay House, Inc., 2010).*

Shelley Moore, (2016). *One without the Other: Stories of unity through diversity and inclusion*. (Winnipeg, MB: Portage and Main Press, 2016).

Susie Wise, *Design for Belonging: how to build inclusion and collaboration in your communities.* Emeryville, (CA: Ten Speed Press, 2022).

Zaid Hassan, The Social Labs Fieldbook, (San Francisco: Berrett-Koehler Publishers, 2014)

Websites

Roots of Attachment public webinar *https://neufeldinstitute.org/resources/free/*

https://www.oxfordlearnersdictionaries.com/definition/english/buzzword

http://www.wannabeteacher.com

http://interactioninstitute.org/illustrating-equality-vs-equity/

https://dschool.stanford.edu/how-to-start-a-dschool/

YouTube

Shelley Moore: The Evolution of Inclusion - *https://www.youtube.com/watch?v=PQgXBhPh5Zo*

Shelley Moore, "Transforming Inclusive Education," April 4, 2016, presentation, 3:08, *https://www.youtube.com/watch?v=RYtUlU8MjlY.*

Shelley Moore, "Under the Table: The Importance of Presuming Competence," March 11, 2016, presentation, 15:11, *https://www.youtube.com/watch?v=AGptAXTV7m0.*

https://klipland.com/video/teacher-punishes-kid-for-being-late-to-school-then-he-finds-the-truth

Sir Ken Robinson: The Changing Paradigm of Education: *https://www.ted.com/talks/sir ken robinson changing education paradigms.*

https://www.educationmattersmag.com.au/the-changing-paradigm-of-education/#:~:text=Changing%20Education%20Paradigms%20is%20a,the%20current%20industrial%20concept%20of

Documents and Publications

Alberta Education, *Superintendent Leadership Quality Standard,* (Edmonton, Alberta: Alberta Education, 2020), *https://open.alberta.ca/publications/superintendent-leadership-quality-standard-2020*

https://www.alberta.ca/guide-to-education.aspx

Alberta's Commission on Learning, *Every child learns Every child succeeds: report and recommendations,* (Edmonton, Alberta: 2003), *https://open.alberta.ca/publications/0778526003*

Alberta Education, *Standards for Special Education, amended 2004*, (Edmonton: Learning, 2004), *https://open.alberta.ca/publications/0778537781*

As an example of the companion documents: Alberta Education, *Essential components of educational programming for students who are blind or visually impaired [2004]* (Edmonton, Alberta: 2004), *https://open.alberta.ca/publications/0778543226*

Setting the Direction Framework June 2009 https://files.eric.ed.gov/fulltext/ED506091.pdf

Alberta Education, *Ministerial Order #028/2020 [Education]: Student learning,* (Edmonton, Alberta: Alberta Education, 2020), *https://open.alberta.ca/publications/ministerial-order-on-student-learning-2020*

Alberta Education, *Implementing a Continuum of Supports and Services: A Resource Guide for School and School Authority Leaders*, (Edmonton, Alberta: Alberta Education, 2022), 12.

Report of the Blue-Ribbon Panel on Inclusive Education in Alberta Schools (2014), (The Alberta Teachers Association, Edmonton, 2014), *https://legacy.teachers.ab.ca/SiteCollectionDocuments/*

ATA/Publications/Professional-Development/PD-170-1%20 PD%20Blue%20Ribbon%20Panel%20Report.pdf

Alberta Education, *Working together: collaborative practices and partnership toolkit: supporting Alberta Students,* (Edmonton: Alberta Education, 2013), *https://open.alberta.ca/ dataset/6927719-english.*

Alberta Education, *Shaping the Future for Students with Special Education Needs: A Review,* (Edmonton, Alberta: Alberta Learning, 2000).

The CASSCONNECTION: The official magazine for the College of Alberta School Superintendents, vol. 15, issue 2, Fall 2019, 16-17

The CASSCONNECTION: The official magazine for the College of Alberta School Superintendents, vol. 12, issue 2, Fall 2016 17-19

Zaid Hassan, The Social Labs Fieldbook, (San Francisco: Berrett-Koehler Publishers, 2014),

https://social-labs.org/fieldbook/

Isaac Newton, *Letter from Sir Isaac Newton to Robert Hooke* (Historical Society of Pennsylvania; retrieved 7 June, 2018).

K. Hilton and A. Anderson, *IHI Psychology of Change Framework to Advance and Sustain Improvement,* (Boston, Massachusetts: Institute for Healthcare Improvement; 2018) *https://www.ihi.org/ resources/Pages/IHIWhitePapers/IHI-Psychology-of-Change-Framework.aspx*

Heather Graham and Linda Mollenhauer, *Participating Effectively as a Collaborative Partner: A United Way Toronto Toolkit* (Toronto, Ontario: United Way Toronto, 2011),

Manufactured by Amazon.ca
Acheson, AB

13053590R00070